Wm. Lawson

THE
CHRISTIAN
MAN

LAYMAN'S THEOLOGICAL LIBRARY
ROBERT MCAFEE BROWN, *General Editor*

The
Christian
Man

by
William Hamilton

LAYMAN'S
THEOLOGICAL
LIBRARY

THE WESTMINSTER PRESS

PHILADELPHIA

The Scripture quotations in this publication are from the Revised Standard Version of the Bible, copyrighted, 1946 and 1952, by the Division of Christian Education of the National Council of Churches, and used by permission.

Acknowledgment is made for permission to quote from the following:
"The Rock," from *Collected Poems of T. S. Eliot.* Copyright, 1934, 1936, by Harcourt, Brace and Company, Inc.
"Under Which Lyre," from *Nones,* by W. H. Auden. Copyright, 1946, by W. H. Auden.
Faith, Sex, and Love, by William Hamilton. Published by the National Student Council of the Y.M.C.A. and Y.W.C.A.
"A Christian Theology in Miniature," by William Hamilton. Published in *The Intercollegian,* the monthly journal of the National Student Y.M.C.A. and Y.W.C.A.
Too Late the Phalarope, by Alan Paton. Charles Scribner's Sons, 1953.

Library of Congress Catalog Card No.: 56–8666

PRINTED IN THE UNITED STATES OF AMERICA

CONTENTS

FOREWORD

The religious book market is full of books for "the intelligent layman." Some are an insult to his intelligence. Others are covertly written for professional theologians. A few are genuine helps in communicating the faith.

In this spate of books being thrust at the lay reader, what distinctive place can the Layman's Theological Library claim to hold? For one thing, it will try to remind the layman that he *is* a theologian. The close conjunction of the words "layman" and "theological" in the title of the series is not by chance but by design. For theology is not an irrelevant pastime of seminary professors. It is the occupation of every Christian, the moment he begins to think about, or talk about, or communicate, his Christian faith. The injunction to love God *with all his mind,* necessarily involves the layman in theology. He can never avoid theology; if he refuses to think through his faith, he simply settles for an inferior theology.

Furthermore, the Layman's Theological Library will attempt to give a *wholeness* in its presentation of the Christian faith. Its twelve volumes cover the main areas of Christian faith and practice. They are written out of similar convictions, which the authors share, about the uniqueness of the Christian faith. All the authors are convinced that Christian faith can be made relevant, that it can be made understandable without becom-

7

ing innocuous, and that (particularly in view of the current
" return to religion ") it is crucially important for the layman
to commit himself to more than " religion in general." The
Layman's Theological Library, then, will attempt a fresh ex-
ploration of the Christian faith and what it can mean in the
life of twentieth-century man.

Many people are not too clear about God, or Christ, or
eternal life, but at least they know something about themselves.
To be sure, many of the things they know about themselves
may be wrong, or at best inadequate; but to ask, " Who am I?
What makes me the way I am?" is a clear place to start the
pilgrimage toward Christian faith.

The present book is designed for such people. Rather than
beginning with abstract definitions, the author helps the reader
see what it means to be a man by confronting him with a
Man. And in the light of that analysis, not only will the reader's understanding of himself be illumined, but also his understanding of his fellow men and of Christ. The latter part of
the book retraces the ground by taking one aspect of human
life, sexuality, and finding from that aspect further confirmation of the truth and relevance of the Christian analysis of human nature. The appendix furnishes some tools for a deeper
understanding of the Biblical context of the problem.

If we begin with man, we do not end with man, as the author shows so well. We end with God and find, when all is
said and done, that we really began with him also.

ROBERT McAFEE BROWN

CHAPTER

1

STARTING POINT

The subject of this book is sometimes called "the Christian doctrine of man." This abstract language is not only vague but dangerous. It is not true that our faith provides us with some kind of secret information about the true nature of other people.

What is really meant when the Christian doctrine of man is discussed is this: as Christians, we are given a new kind of *self*-understanding. Faith provides us with a unique insight into our own hearts. When we talk about sin, for example, we are far from the truth if we think Christians are experts on the sins of other people. Actually, we probably have no right to make an estimate of the sin of anyone else but ourselves. But we do come to understand ourselves and our sin in a new way in the light of faith. To make clear how this happens is the task of the Christian doctrine of man.

The self-understanding that faith brings is not a substitute for the other ways in which we may learn about ourselves or the world. We are not exempt from the responsibility of learning from the secular studies of man. We may still read books of psychology, or novels, or modern poetry, or Sherlock Holmes, or Mickey Spillane. From any of these, some insight into man's foolishness or wisdom may come, and we are never so sure of ourselves that we can afford to look down on secular learning. But, beyond what all these can provide, we must still try to claim that our Christian faith says a distinctive word about man that we cannot find being said anywhere else.

If we go to the modern theological studies on " the doctrine of man," we will find that almost all of them are extended elaborations on some such theme as this: " The Christian is a creature made in the image of God. But he has fallen from this high status into sin, through his rebellion and pride." " Creature," " image of God," " Fall," " sin," " pride " — these are the key words generally used in Christian writing about man today. But notice one thing about them. They are largely derived from the Old Testament story of the Fall of man in Gen., ch. 3. (A brief study of Gen., ch. 3, is provided in an appendix at the end of this book.) Now there are many advantages in using this Old Testament language, but there is one real danger. The unique understanding of man that we are looking for is, after all, a Christian thing; and it is therefore true that, however helpful and revealing it may be for us to read Gen., ch. 3, as the story of our lives, the first and central place we go for self-understanding — as Christians — is to the New Testament. Here we are reminded that the distinctive mark of the Christian man is not a certain kind of behavior, not belief, not even faith in God; it is a unique relationship to Jesus Christ, the Lord.

So we must ask: What does this unique Christian relationship tell us about ourselves? Just what does happen to us when we come up against Jesus Christ?

CHRIST'S DOUBLE DEMAND

Whether Christ comes to a man as the very beginning of his religious life, or whether he comes to the mature and disciplined Christian, *Christ comes first with a demand*. And it is a demand that sets up in us a serious and often costly kind of self-questioning. Even the most cursory reader of the gospel story is unable to avoid the impression of an authoritative and demanding person. (We are talking about the Christ of the Gospels now, and not the Christ of popular illustration or song. It may be true that " He walks with me, and He talks with me, And He tells me I am His own"; but the sentimental and almost erotic flavor of this hymn can be misleading if we do not see that we must meet his demand before we can have any peace with him.) Before Peter could be the " rock," the courageous and eloquent leader of the Early Church, he had to learn to say, " Depart from me, for I am a sinful man, O Lord " (Luke 5:8). And if we have never wanted to get out of being Christian, if we have never been tempted to evade the disturbance of Christ by denying him altogether, we have never really known him as he is. To be sure, he comes to sinners; but, when he comes to sinners like ourselves, he makes us very uneasy about our sin. The demanding Christ means that the Christian is first of all a discontented man, a man without peace.

There is, first, *the demand of his life.* If we look at his life honestly, and then look at our own, something shattering is bound to happen.

" He was careless about himself, we are careful. He was courageous, we are cautious. He trusted the untrustworthy, we trust those who have good collateral. He forgave the unforgivable, we forgive those who do not really hurt us. He was righteous and laughed at respectability, we are respectable and smile at righteousness. He was meek, we are ambitious. He saved others, we save ourselves as much as we can. He had no place to lay his head, and did not worry about it, while we fret because we do not have the last convenience manufactured by clever science. He did what he believed to be right regardless of consequences, while we determine what is right by how it will affect us. He feared God, but not the world. We fear public opinion more than we fear the judgment of God. He risked everything for God, we make religion a refuge from every risk." (Samuel H. Miller, *The Life of the Church,* pp. 46, 47.)

Is this *really* true of Christ? All we can do is refer to the evidence. When the disciples were arguing about which of them was the greatest, Jesus set a child in the midst of them as a mark of the kind of character the Kingdom of God required (Luke 9:46–48). When a man wished briefly to put his own affairs in order before he came to follow Jesus, Jesus uttered a severe rebuke: " No one who puts his hand to the plow and looks back is fit for the kingdom of God " (v. 62). And there was the young man who asked how he could inherit eternal life. He claimed to have followed all the Commandments, so he asked what more was needed. Jesus then put to him the supreme test: " Sell all that you have and distribute to the poor, . . . and come, follow me." The young man reacted in a way that must seem to us very natural: he turned away sadly. (Ch. 18:18–23.)

The demand of Jesus' life is the uncomfortable one that we should be like him: our obedience, our humility, our selflessness should be like his own.

What can we do with this radical demand of his life? Several things. We can, of course, reject it. This is perhaps the easiest way out. We can reject it by denying that this portrait is really an accurate one, by building up for ourselves a more manageable version of Christ, more harmless, less bothersome, easier to follow. We can make a more honest rejection by saying that if this is what the Christ of the Gospels is like, we will have none of him. After all, let's be honest. This is too much to ask of modern man. We have a far more complex life than he had; he failed to take into account so many important complicating factors. No, we can say, we will look for some meaning to our lives that will be a little easier on us.

Or, on the other hand, we can accept the demand of Christ. Granting what we may call the impossibility of his life, we may still say: " This demand is placed upon us as men of faith. It may show us up as tragically wanting and inept. But somehow we cannot modify either its radicalism or its relevance to us." This kind of acceptance still leaves its problems and we shall have to look at some of them later on in this book, but surely the Christian is one who tries to read the life of Christ in this final way.

But there is more to this demanding Christ. If the life of Christ is a powerful blow to our self-satisfaction, so is his teaching. Let us look, then, at *the demand of his teaching*. American Protestantism has sometimes tried to believe that the Gospels enshrine the " simple " Jesus, easy to understand and easy to follow, while Paul and the Early Church came in and confused things needlessly with their queer speculations about the Son of God and the atoning death on the cross.

But this simple, idyllic teacher does not exist. Let us examine some of the so-called " simple teachings." Let us take the first part of the Sermon on the Mount. Everyone admires the Sermon on the Mount. Even politicians and newspapermen come out strongly in its favor at appropriate seasons during the year. Hardly anyone can be found to be against it. Many feel that it represents the only thing necessary for the moral and religious life. Mr. Truman once stated that his foreign policy was based on it; Mr. J. C. Penney said the same of his business practices. Strange that two men who would probably agree on little else could agree on this. Can such claims stand? We can find out only by reading Matt., chs. 5 to 7, carefully. When we do, we will find that they contain the same radical demand that we found in the life of Christ. The Sermon on the Mount is more accurately described as a criticism of all foreign policy (even the best) and a terrible judgment on all business practices (even the most enlightened). Far from being a simple guide for our conventional moral behavior, it criticizes and very nearly destroys it.

Sören Kierkegaard, the lonely and eccentric Danish thinker of the last century, somewhere says that the way to become a Christian is to take any one of Jesus' teaching precepts and try to follow it. He did not mean that it would be so easy that we would all at once become convinced Christians. He meant that, if we really tried to follow any particular teaching, we would be driven, in the first instance, to a confession of unworthiness, to a broken and contrite heart. And the Christian faith can begin in no other way.

Is this sheer perversity, or is there some truth in it?

Beginning at Matt. 5:21, Jesus sets his teaching over against the interpretation of the Old Testament law that the scribes were making, taking some of their characteristic moral teachings and probing into their deepest meaning. Let us look at what is going on.

"You have heard that it was said to the men of old, 'You shall not kill; and whoever kills shall be liable to judgment.' But I say to you that every one who is angry with his brother shall be liable to judgment; whoever insults his brother shall be liable to the council, and whoever says, 'You fool!' shall be liable to the hell of fire." (Ch. 5:21, 22.)

The scribes in your midst today, Jesus says to his disciples, are interpreting Moses' commandment "Thou shalt not kill" in its simple literal sense. They tell you that you are fulfilling the Commandment so long as you avoid what society calls killing or murder. Then comes his startling claim to authority, "But I say to you." What is the real meaning of killing? What is the inner psychological disposition of the heart that can lead to murder? Is it not anger? Is it not the almost natural and everyday tendency of the human heart to elevate itself, to make itself superior, by making critical judgments of another?

So while the scribes simply prohibit the external act of killing, Jesus insists that we cannot have a good conscience merely by avoiding the outer act. God's demand here is that we avoid the inner disposition that can lead to murder: anger; saying to someone you do not like, "You fool"; inflicting a thoughtless insult that wounds the other and gives us a sense of superiority and victory. *God's will is that our inner motive be as pure as our outer act.* Many of us might come off pretty well if obedience to the Commandment simply meant the avoidance of killing, but are we quite so secure when we see the inner meaning that Jesus here reveals? Have we not broken this Commandment — as Jesus interprets it — daily?

Or again Jesus says, and even more vividly:

"You have heard that it was said, 'You shall not commit

adultery.' But I say to you that every one who looks at a woman lustfully has already committed adultery with her in his heart." (Ch. 5:27, 28.)

The scribes are interpreting the Commandment against adultery to mean that the man who has avoided the act which society defines as adultery can claim to have fulfilled the law and, at that point at least, can have a clear conscience. But again a clear conscience is denied us by Jesus' probing. What is that inner motive, that inner movement of the human heart which, under certain conditions, leads to the act of adultery? It is what Jesus calls looking at a woman lustfully. Again, from the outer act he probes inward to the egoism of the human heart. The selfish desire to impose one's own body on the body of another — it is this desire that is prohibited by God, and not simply the outer act. And while some of us might be able to claim exemption to the scribes' interpretation of this law, does Jesus' reinterpretation of it let any of us off? Are we not all adulterers? It is hard to see that any other meaning can be given to the passage. This does not mean that inward lust is morally equivalent to the act of adultery. But it does mean that God wills restraint and discipline in both the external sexual act and the inner psychological attitude.

We can now see the kind of thinking that is involved in this particular section of the apparently " simple " Sermon on the Mount. The meaning of the Old Testament law is not found merely in the observance of external forms of behavior. God demands a particular kind of inner attitude as well; our *motives* as well as our acts are to be controlled by him. Jesus is here demanding moral conduct without permitting us to consider how the other person will act. " You, therefore, must be perfect, as your heavenly Father is perfect," he says at the end of the section we have been studying (ch. 5:48). This demand **is not** based **on** practicability, on possible consequences, on what others might do. It is based on God, on what he is like, what he has done. Anything short of this kind of moral character is short of God's will for us.

This is the demand of Jesus' teaching. We have here something far different from a series of simple techniques for Christian living. Here is rather an undistorted mirror by which we may see our distortion, a probing scalpel that reveals our inner disease. We have a means by which we can look at ourselves in the light of God. And we do not like what we see. We are, Christians say, sinners. This means that when we first confront the life and teaching of Jesus Christ, we cannot find the rest and peace we expected to find. However decent we may consider ourselves (and we may be quite decent), however highly others estimate us (and they may estimate us very highly), the life and teaching of Jesus Christ provide a standard that does not let us off so easily. We begin to be aware of a disturbance that this encounter with Christ has set up. We now understand what Peter meant when he cried, " Leave us alone," or " Depart from me, for I am a sinful man." This disturbance is the true beginning of the Christian man's understanding of himself.

If this demand were the only note of the Christian faith, however, it would be a most inadequate faith indeed. Demand, judgment, probing, bewilderment, hostility, uneasiness, unworthiness — these are not the final marks of the Christian man, but they are his first marks. The Sermon on the Mount is not the gospel, the good news; it is bad news. But beyond the demand of Christ there is a gift.

The Strange Fact of Forgiveness

No man speaks more passionately than Paul of the gift of forgiveness that Christ makes possible. But before he could speak of that, he had to feel Christ's agonizing and costly demand. In ch. 7 of the Epistle to the Romans he deals with the same issue we saw to be the key to Matt., ch. 5: the relation of law (or, as we would say, moral principles or values) to the Christian life. For Paul, the law was impossible as a guide — he could not live up to its demand. But he did find it extremely valuable, indeed essential, in bringing him to an awareness of his sin. So the law is partly evil in that it cannot be the total basis for faith, but partly good because it directs man to discover his own sin. When Paul (in Gal. 3:24, K.J.V.) describes the law as a " schoolmaster " leading men to Christ, we ought to think of a harsh and ruthless taskmaster rather than an enlightened modern teacher.

Paul is baffled when he sees what the demand of Christ really involves. " I can will what is right, but I cannot do it " (Rom. 7:18). The good is perfectly clear to him, but this knowledge of the good is not much help. " For I do not do the good I want, but the evil I do not want is what I do " (v. 19). We need, he is saying, something more than knowledge of the good. For even when we know this we find ourselves doing what we really don't want to do, and leaving undone what we really want to do. This becomes a real struggle, a kind of despair, for Paul:

" For I delight in the law of God, in my inmost self, but I see in my members another law at war with the law of my mind and making me captive to the law of sin which dwells in my members. Wretched man that I am! Who will deliver me from this body of death? [This is where the demand of Christ leaves men; but there is a second half to the Christian story. There is something beyond the demand.] Thanks be to God through Jesus Christ our Lord! So then, I of myself serve the law of God with my mind, but with my flesh [with my total self insofar as it is separated from God] I serve the law of sin. (Ch. 7:22–25.)

Notice the alternation between the cry of despair, the exclamation of thanks to God, and again the description of struggle at the end.

As this passage continues Paul describes somewhat more precisely what it is that lies behind the gift of the gospel. How, we might ask, is the disturbance and uneasy conscience of the man confronted by Christ's terrible demand to be relieved?

" There is therefore now no condemnation for those who are in Christ Jesus. For the law of the Spirit of life in Christ Jesus has set me free from the law of sin and death. For God has done what the law, weakened by the flesh, could not do: sending his own Son in the likeness of sinful flesh and for sin, he condemned sin in the flesh, in order that the just requirement of the law might be fulfilled in us, who walk not according to the flesh but according to the Spirit." (Ch. 8:1–4.)

Paul makes it quite clear that beyond the disturbing demand there is the gift. But what does all this really mean? What can we say about the Christian man except that he is a sinner?

Is he something more besides? Is he also pure, virtuous, righteous, holy?

No, the sinner is always a sinner in this life. So long as we are human, the demand of Christ will have its judging and probing work to do. But the gift of Jesus Christ means that we are something more. The Christian is also a *forgiven* sinner.

Forgiveness of sins: there is not much more to the Christian gospel than this. But what does it mean to say that the man of faith is not only faced by a demand but also a gift, and that this gift can be described as forgiveness of sins? What does it mean to say that God can forgive sins? And how is this related to the life and death of Jesus Christ which we are so often assured has something to do with the forgiveness of sins?

It is very important to see forgiveness as part of the Christian's understanding of himself; apart from it we are simply sinners and no more. With it, we are forgiven sinners, and everything is changed. Three remarks will make this a little clearer.

1. We will never understand the meaning of *divine* forgiveness unless we distinguish between true and false forgiveness on the *human* level. We often couple the words " forgive " and " forget." But true human forgiveness does not mean a good-natured forgetting, an easy passing aside of some wrong done.

Let us suppose that you and I work in the same office and have always been close friends. In order to secure a promotion and to win favor with my boss, imagine that I have willfully circulated a vicious and totally untrue rumor about the moral character of your father, a " Have you heard . . . ? " whisper at the water cooler. My lie is found out, and as a result our friendship is gravely threatened. Can it be restored? Would forgiveness be possible between us?

Perhaps I might come to you, genuinely sorry for what I had

done, honestly wanting to restore our broken relationship, asking you to hear me out and to forgive. One of the things you simply could not do, if our relationship meant anything, would be to say glibly: "Of course I forgive you, don't worry about it any more." This would neither be fair to your father, nor to the depth of our relationship. If you really wanted to forgive me, you would have to show me that my act had deeply hurt and troubled you. Your being hurt would have to affect me. I would have to see that your forgiveness was a difficult thing for you to offer honestly. But if you did win through to a willingness to restore our relationship, then that costly forgiveness could mean something to me. Your accepting me could begin to help me accept myself.

All this is just a reminder that *the divine forgiveness of which the Gospel speaks is a costly thing for God*. He is not merely a half-blind father who will forgive in some automatic way whenever asked. Christians have always claimed that the love and forgiveness of God are most poignantly revealed in the death of Jesus Christ on the cross. Here is not merely the suffering love of a noble man, not merely Jesus' forgiveness of his enemies, but God himself, bearing to the full the cost of the sin that crucified his Son, and still, even as he is judging us, offering us forgiveness and love. When we see how costly real forgiveness must be in our deepest human relationships, we can never make it an easy thing for God.

2. Forgiveness will never make sense unless we understand that *in the life and death of Jesus Christ, God himself was acting for us*. Jesus does not merely teach about a God who forgives; he forgives sin himself. He looks at the paralytic carried by his friends and says, "My son, your sins are forgiven" (Mark 2:5). Some of the Jews, hearing this, accused Jesus of blasphemy, for they believed that God alone could forgive sins. Later, at the trial before the Jewish court, blasphemy is the

very charge made against him: he claims to do what God alone can do. And this is exactly what we claim today about Jesus Christ. In him we have far more than a pointer to a distant God; we have God himself in the midst of men, healing broken bodies and minds, announcing the Kingdom of God. The demand of Christ is the demand of God; the gift, the forgiveness of Christ, is the gift or grace of God.

3. Finally, we ought to remember that *the centrality of the gospel of forgiveness is what makes us Protestants.* Distrust any part of theology, Martin Luther used to say, that cannot be reduced to the forgiveness of sins. As a matter of fact, Luther was led to his protest against the distortions of medieval religion precisely because it had obscured this central truth.

"What is forgiveness? How can I deserve a God who will forgive me?" These were the agonizing questions that the young Luther asked himself when he entered the monastery to begin his religious training. God seemed to him a terrible sort of being — remote, yet demanding such perfection of his creatures. The phrase "righteousness of God" was the chief thing that bothered Luther. He had always interpreted this to mean the goodness or righteousness God requires from us before he will come to us. God will forgive us, Luther first felt, only when we have become worthy of that forgiveness. But Luther found that he simply could not achieve this sense of worthiness. He fasted, he worked doubly hard on his religious exercises in the monastery, but still a sense of his own worthiness did not come. "I hate, I despise this God," he would cry out, "this God who asks something I cannot fulfill, who demands that I become righteous before he will forgive me."

What happened then was very simple. Luther returned to his Bible and suddenly saw that he had missed its central meaning completely. "The righteousness of God" did not there refer to a vain monarch requiring obedience. It referred to a loving Father who forgives us in the midst of our unrighteousness. The demanding God, he found, was not the last word of the Bible. The forgiving God who gives, through a relationship to him, the very righteousness he demands — this he saw to be the deepest truth of the gospel. That Luther was led to protest against the medieval system which had lost this truth was almost incidental to the prior fact that this new insight into an old truth saved him from despair. Forgiveness, he saw, meant that our disobedience, doubt, despair, are not insuperable obstacles for God's access to us. God can plunge through all of these to come to us, and we can receive him simply by confessing our need.

Protestantism was born when God forgave Martin Luther. And it is revitalized whenever we grasp the wonder of that forgiveness for ourselves.

CHAPTER

4

WHAT DIFFERENCE DOES FORGIVENESS MAKE?

We have noted some specific effects of the demand of Christ: a sense of unworthiness, resentment, bewilderment, inadequacy. Are there equally specific effects deriving from the gift of God's forgiveness? Does the Christian as such have any distinguishing characteristic marks about him? What does he do, how does he act, how is he different, as a Christian?

Now it is easy to get into all kinds of trouble answering these questions. The greatest danger is that the Christian will be so sure about his own virtue, and will call attention to it so eagerly, that what is left is not a Christian at all but a prig. But, dangerous or not, the questions still call for an answer. Here is one attempt. *The Christian man has a new perspective on the decisions he has to make; he has a new freedom which is his most distinguishing mark; and he is able to call upon the life and teaching of Jesus Christ as his norm or pattern.* Because of the gift of forgiveness, the encounter with Christ which initially troubled the Christian can now be a creative one. The individual's " Depart from me " is now matched by Christ's " Come to me." Let us examine the three parts of the statement italicized above.

1. What does it mean to say that the Christian man, the for-

24

given sinner, is given a new "perspective"?

Many of the daily decisions we make are neither simple nor obvious. In the discipline of children, in the conflict between personal integrity and the desire for success, in weighing military service and conscientious objection, in deciding to join a fraternity at college — in each alternative there is a mixture of the good and the less than good. We never confront a clearly drawn choice between pure evil and pure good, except perhaps in the wrestling matches and the soap operas on television. (Is this the reason these so fascinate us, often against our wills? Because virtue always wins, and it is soothing to be reminded that there is some place left where this is true?) So our daily life always requires us to make choices that have some evil in them, in order to do more of the good.

Let us imagine a family discussing the question of their son's joining a fraternity at college, trying to bring their Christian faith to bear on the problem. On the one hand is the fact that many fraternities have written or unwritten prohibitions against Negroes, Jews, and sometimes Roman Catholics. This is obviously a vicious thing, opposed both to human decency and to the Christian faith. Is the Christian word to the young man just going to college therefore a no to fraternities? It may be that such a no would mean loneliness, being deprived of the main stream of social life and friendship. Are we simply to say that if we are Christians we should be willing to bear this for the sake of our faith?

Let us look at the other side. Granted, the fraternity system is bad at best and intolerable at worst. But is it quite so obviously the case that the Christian should stay away from it so his hands won't get dirty? Perhaps the really Christian action would be to join, if possible, and to fight against the injustice of the system from within, where one is more likely to be effective.

We have to watch ourselves carefully here. We may be in danger of giving high-sounding Christian reasons for doing what we wanted to do: follow the stream, join a fraternity like everyone else. And there are many illusions about the ease with which the struggle against the injustices in the fraternity system can be carried on. It seems to be clear that on this matter a simple Christian yes or no is impossible. The Christian cannot avoid responsibility for the injustice by staying out of the system. This would mean that he would be allowing the fight to be carried on by others so he could maintain his own virtue. But just as certainly he cannot join a fraternity without being fully aware of the falseness and stupidity of much of what goes on. Sometimes, it may be, a no is the best answer; sometimes it may not be. Whatever is done in each particular situation will not be perfectly good. It will be a partial and imperfect decision at best. This is what is meant by saying that the ordinary decisions of our lives require forgiveness of sins.

We must choose, we must act, however imperfectly. In such situations, forgiveness of sins does give us a perspective within which decisions involving some necessary evil can be made without despair and without self-deception.

2. Secondly, the forgiven sinner is given a *freedom* through the gospel of forgiveness. In Christ we are made truly free.

What exactly does this mean? One thing can be said. Through the forgiveness of sins, through the word that comes to us from God through Christ, we become freed from all fussy concern about ourselves and how our personalities are getting along, freed from worry about how others think of us. Now this freedom from concern about what others think is a very precious thing indeed, but it is not an irresponsible thing. We are free *from* ourselves and free *for* service to God and our neighbor. We are free from ourselves precisely because we no longer have to put absolute confidence in ourselves. Our confidence, our trust, our faith is in God and in what he is do-ing for us. When I realize that I do not have to be my own god, I can take myself far less seriously and lose most of the petty worries that usually cluster around the person who can-not learn this freedom.

All this means is that the Christian ought to be far more marked by flexibility, lightness of touch, humor, than he usu-ally is. His character ought to be far more unconventional and unpredictable than it has usually been. When Augustine wrote, " Love God, and do what you like," he was uttering a very dangerous remark, but one describing quite accurately the kind of freedom that is available to the Christian if he wants to make use of it. If you really love God, he means, you can be trusted to do what you like. The " you " involved will be a " you " which loves God, and therefore a responsible " you." Professor Herbert Butterfield asks if there is a single lesson than can guide the believer through the tangled prob-lems of past and present. He concludes that there *is* a maxim that contains both the stability and flexibility we need. It is this: " Hold to Christ, and for the rest be totally uncommit-ted." (*Christianity and History*, p. 146.)

Love God, hold to Christ — these phrases point to the only grounds for Christian certainty. We are not certain of very much as Christians; above all, our certainty does not rest in ourselves. But we do claim to hold to a God who can be trusted. We say this because he has been trustworthy with us; he has treated us far beyond our deserts; he has given himself to us in Christ. We are not free, *as Christians,* to reject Christ. If we hold to him, and hold absolutely to nothing else, we can know a genuine freedom in our lives that is one of the most valuable and attractive gifts of the Christian faith.

W. H. Auden portrays nicely this sort of reverent rebellious-ness. We need not agree with his detailed prejudices (though

we may) to observe that this is a real blow for the right kind
of religious posture before the world.

> " Thou shalt not do as the dean pleases,
>   Thou shalt not write thy doctor's thesis
>   On education,
>   Thou shalt not worship projects nor
>   Shalt thou or thine bow down before
>   Administration.
>
> " Thou shalt not answer questionnaires
>   Or quizzes upon World-Affairs,
>   Nor with compliance
>   Take any test. Thou shalt not sit
>   With statisticians nor commit
>   A social science.
>
> " Thou shalt not be on friendly terms
>   With guys in advertising firms,
>   Nor speak with such
>   As read the Bible for its prose,
>   Nor, above all, make love to those
>   Who wash too much.
>
> " Thou shalt not live within thy means
>   Nor on plain water and raw greens.
>   If thou must choose
>   Between the chances, choose the odd;
>   Read *The New Yorker*, trust in God;
>   And take short views."
>   (" Under Which Lyre," in *Nones.*)

In all these statements there is a charter of Christian liberty
if we only knew how to claim it. Notice that the freedom
comes from a profound and thorough trust in God. He can

be trusted for the future, so we will concern ourselves simply with serving him today. And if our service to him is as faithful and complete as we can make it, then we need not worry about how we look to anyone else.

3. Finally, the forgiven sinner can turn back to the life, character, and teaching of Christ, and can make use of them in a new way. When Christ first made his approach, it was as radical demand. We saw that we needed something besides the law or moral rules to live by. The rules alone condemned us. But as forgiven sinners who have received the healing word of acceptance and power from God, we can rise from our knees to re-appropriate the life and teaching of Christ in a fresh way. That which first made such a probing demand can now become a pattern that sustains and gives definite content and guidance to the work we have to do in the world. The life and teaching of Christ, once a pointer directing us to our own unworthiness, now points to something else: away from ourselves to the service of our neighbor.

Let us take an example of this. When we read in Matt. 5:44 that the disciple is to love his enemies, we first see that we cannot. This demand reveals the vast complex of hostilities that all of us live with: noisy neighbors across the street, the Russians, the stupid Republicans or the witless Democrats. But when we take this demand as a judgment of God on our imperfect obedience to him, when we come to him as sinners confessing that we do not come anywhere near to loving our enemies or even our friends, we can then become at least honest enough with ourselves to let God get at us with his terrible and forgiving love. When he has forgiven us, we can never again be as sure of the evil of our enemies (or of our own virtue) as we once were. We will continue to fight for our political views, to criticize our political opponents as before.

But our basic attitude to the opponent or enemy is decisively changed. We are much closer together than before, because we are both sinners under God, both needing his healing and changing. We will oppose our " enemy " now with much greater understanding of why he stands where he stands, with much more sensitivity to the pressures under which he operates. We will oppose him still, when we must do so, but without reducing him to a subhuman level. When politicians refer to the struggle against subversives in government as a rat hunt, they make a statement about their enemies that is morally degenerate and deeply un-Christian. Jesus says love your enemies. This is both a demand that reveals our sin, and a practical safety valve and guide for our lives. It is impossible in that we cannot perfectly do it. But it is also relevant in that it can be a goal that informs all our personal and political controversy.

The life and teaching of Jesus Christ, then, no longer simply drive us to despondency, for we can be forgiven by God when we confess our daily failure to him. But if we are not made despondent by the demand of Christ, neither are we permitted self-righteousness. Forgiveness has not given us virtue of which we may boast. It has only given us God. As soon as we boast that we deserve forgiveness, we are condemned again. This is the normal rhythm of the life of the Christian: contrition, forgiveness, obedience. When we come to build this rhythm into our lives, we may understand a little better Christ's promise that while his disciples must wear a yoke, it is an easy one. The Christian life is perhaps a burden; but it is light, for we do not carry it alone.

A Portrait of Christian Man

Forgiveness, then, does make a difference. The Christian as forgiven sinner does have something unique and characteristic in his life. Another way of putting this is to say that there is such a thing as a distinctive Christian character. If the gospel has really begun to do its transforming work, there will be a particular flavor and style to the Christian life. We have already begun to describe this in terms of a new relationship to Christ and in terms of freedom. Let us try to sketch out more fully the meaning of this elusive character or style of life.

We can see it in contrast with other character types: the self-sufficient man of the self-help books, the leisurely gentleman of the magazine ads, the much-criticized suburban conformist in gray flannel, the equally conforming Bohemian in blue jeans. It is different from all of these, though something of each of these may be in a finished Christian portrait.

As a matter of fact, the Christian character is not easily set down in a list of rules and precepts. It is really a combination of opposites: confidence and humility, " wise as serpents and innocent as doves," sorrowful yet always rejoicing, stern with oneself yet charitable toward the failings of others, separate from sinners and yet friend of sinners, both this-worldly and other-worldly. This distinctive character or style really comes

alive in the actual man Jesus Christ. No list of virtues or precepts, but a man, is the norm of Christian character. Christ is
the proper man, man as he ought to be.

And we can find in the gospel story such a picture of Christ.
We see him living a real human life in the villages and on the
roads of Galilee. We see him leaving his home as a young man
to be baptized by John, there hearing his call to a public ministry. We see him wrestling with real temptation to choose an
easy way that will guarantee success. We see one who cared
for ordinary people, gathering around him a group of working men; we cannot miss the compassion for sufferers, the interest in outcasts and children. We see one who was very much
at home in crowds, but who astonished his disciples by his
habit of stealing away into solitude to spend long hours in
prayer to God. We see him so gentle and approachable, yet so
stern; so merciful to failures but so intolerant of respectable
hypocrites; so fearless in the face of danger, whether from a
storm on the lake or from human antagonists; so considerate,
yet caring so little what people thought of him; claiming such
absolute allegiance, yet so careless of popularity and reputa-
tion because he claimed nothing for himself, but all for God.

Some such portrait as this certainly emerges from the gospel
story. This is an unexpected kind of character: strange, flexi-
ble, disciplined, yet free. When we meet something like it in
our experience, we unmistakeably recognize it as an authentic
and desirable thing. And any full Christian doctrine of man
ought to include some such attempt to work out a picture of
man as he ought to be, man as Christians believe he can be.

But even if we all agree that this is a good thing, where do
we go from here? What is to keep us from studying this picture of Jesus, minutely examining ourselves in relation to it —
pleased with ourselves when we find success, despondent when
we find shortcoming? What is to keep this approach to the

Christian life from becoming another "law," forcing us to fasten attention on how we measure up? Doesn't this approach still box us up in the old dilemma of self-centeredness that we have been trying all along to shake off?

The curious secret to the whole story is that this Christian character cannot be had by aiming directly at it. It can be grown in us, but only in an atmosphere of faith and trust in God, and only when we are not aware of what is going on. If we try to make ourselves good by seeking to be good, we have not begun to break out of our self-centeredness. *We* are still at the center, searching, trying, worrying about how we are getting along. This self-centered quest for goodness at its best can only turn us into prigs or prudes, forever calling attention to ourselves and our perfection. But the very thing we need to be freed from is self-centeredness, and it is clearly impossible for the self to say to itself that it should not be concerned with the self. Conscious cultivation is the worst possible means for achieving anything like this Christian picture of man.

So what are we to do? If we trust the testimony of those who know something of this authentic Christian character, we discover that the process by which they attain it is quite different from the process of self-conscious striving. As a matter of fact, they don't even call it a method for the attaining of the Christian character at all, for their secret is that they are not thinking primarily of their own character, but of God. Such goodness as emerged in their lives is a goodness that grows freely and unseen as a response to the love of God. The love of God comes through to them and breaks the circle of self-centeredness they have so tightly drawn about themselves, the circle which they cannot themselves break for all their trying to be good.

Jesus' words in Matt. 5:16 speak directly to this problem: "Let your light so shine before men, that they may see your

good works and give glory to your Father who is in heaven."
Now it is relatively easy to "let our light shine" before men
so they will say, "My, what a deeply Christian person he is!"
But this is precisely what is prohibited. Behavior that draws
attention to itself is immoral behavior, however fruitful of results it may be. The problem is how to act as a Christian so
that the glory or credit cannot be given to us, but only to God.

Have you ever done a relatively unselfish thing — gone to
visit a friend in the hospital, for instance? And when you returned to a group of your friends, didn't you notice how difficult it was not to let drop, perhaps unobtrusively, the fact that
you had visited so-and-so, and you're glad to report that she is
getting along nicely? The Christian character means that we
fail whenever we call attention to our own goodness, or whenever others take notice of it and ascribe it to our own virtue.
We are able to be good, we are able to grow into a genuine
Christian character, only when God himself is given the credit,
and when we are willing to do what we do unseen and without reward — unseen, that is, except for God.

Another way of putting this is to say that the Christian
character is quite literally impossible without a regular discipline of prayer to God. The worship of the church and the
private prayer of Christians are not simply optional adjuncts
to the religious life, they are essential marks of it. Because
of this vicious circle of self-centeredness, one can almost say
that it is impossible to become a Christian without prayer;
and, being one, it is impossible to stay one without it. (Another volume in this series, *Prayer and Personal Religion,* by
John Coburn, will deal with this point in detail.)

Let us briefly go back over the ground we have covered up
to this point. It has been claimed that the Christian faith carries with it, among other things, a particular way of looking

at oneself, a certain kind of attitude to oneself. The center of the Christian gospel is the encounter of the Christian with God through Jesus Christ. The prophet who heard the word of God often responded with a confession of his unworthiness; Peter asked the demanding Christ to depart from him — so we also have found that the Christ who first makes his approach to us does not come with comfort. He comes judging our imperfect and compromising manhood. He comes turning his apparently simple and winsome words into knifelike probes that reveal our self-deception and deceit. We are asked to be perfect, and as soon as this demand comes we know we are not and never will be so.

The Christian faith would indeed be dismal news if this approach were the only one made by God-in-Christ to us. But when he has come as judge and critic, then he can also come as Savior. Or as we have put it, after the demand for perfection comes the gift of forgiveness. After he has asked us for righteousness and we have confessed that we have none, he comes to give us the very thing he asked us for. But this is not a virtue we suddenly acquire; it is a relationship that is wholly given by God, a relationship we do not deserve. Because of this relationship we are not merely sinners but *forgiven* sinners, and this added dimension means that a new kind of life is now possible for us.

6

. . . But the Christian Is Still a Sinner

We have been emphasizing the new thing that is added to the Christian life along with the gift of forgiveness. The Christian is a *forgiven* sinner, to be sure. But we must not forget that we are *still sinners,* and perhaps even sinners in a more radical sense than we suspected before forgiveness.

One of the interesting things in Christian thought today is the return to favor of this word " sin." Optimistic modern man thought he had successfully banished it as an unhealthy vestige from those " distorters " of pure religion like Calvin and the Puritans. But it has been rediscovered and made central again. Why?

It is partly because of the rediscovery of the Bible in Protestantism. We are seeing that the Bible is, from beginning to end, a diagnosis of man's sin, and an offer of a prescription to meet that diagnosis. We are learning to see our disobedience in the disobedience that angered the Old Testament prophets; the slowness of the disciples to understand is our slowness; the fear, timidity, and bitterness of men that brought Christ to his death illumine the same traits in us. The Biblical picture does not allow us merely to speak of other men's evil; it shows us our own. And our anti-Semitism, the white man's exploitation of the colored man — all our clever and facile attempts to escape from admitting the terrible equality of all sinners under God have been revealed and condemned by our recovery of the Bible. We are learning to see that we are Biblical men; the Biblical picture of man is a self-portrait of us all.

But the rediscovery of sin has been forced on us by our contemporary history as well. Reading the daily paper has made it impossible to accept inherent goodness and inevitable progress as satisfactory theories to explain observable human behavior. The past history of Nazism and the present history of Communism are not freaks; they require explanation and understanding. So Christians have been forced to look again at the analysis of the depths of human evil that had been lying forgotten in their own tradition.

But what does this word " sin " mean? When we dealt with Jesus' interpretation of the Commandments about murder and adultery in Matt., ch. 5, we found that we had to respond to his words by a confession of our own inadequacy and sin. God's will is violated, sin is committed, when our inner motives and attitudes — and not merely our outer acts — are wrong. " Thou shalt not kill " involves a prohibition of anger; " thou shalt not commit adultery " involves a prohibition of egoistic lust. So it is not possible to identify sin merely with improper external moral behavior. Sin, the New Testament seems to say, grows with special luxuriousness in people who are very careful not to commit what society calls morally bad acts. For it is precisely the good man who is tempted to claim that he is good.

If this is so, just how can we define sin? Let us begin, not with an abstract definition, but with a suggested approach that will enable us to find out the meaning of sin for ourselves. Let us simply say that sin is that kind of character and behavior that Jesus most ruthlessly fights against. This means that our task is not a search for a single word that will explain all sin, but an investigation of the New Testament material that can throw light on Jesus' own approach to man. Here, as everywhere else, we will find that the best theology is that which springs directly from our wrestling with the pages of the Bible. Let us look at three passages in which Jesus talks about the difference between sin and faith. To come to terms with these will be to take a long step toward an understanding of the meaning of sin. In this first passage, Jesus is speaking to the Pharisees.

"What do you think? A man had two sons; and he went to the first and said, 'Son, go and work in the vineyard today.' And he answered, 'I will not'; but afterward he repented and went. And he went to the second and said the same; and he answered, 'I go, sir,' but did not go. Which of the two did the will of his father?" They said, "The first." Jesus said to them, "Truly, I say to you, the tax collectors and the harlots go into the kingdom of God before you. For John came to you in the way of righteousness, and you did not believe him, but the tax collectors and the harlots believed him; and even when you saw it, you did not afterward repent and believe him." (Matt. 21:28–32.)

Notice the distinction between the son who refuses to obey, but changes his mind and goes to work, and the son who says he will obey, but does not. Here Jesus is speaking a slightly veiled word of rebuke to the respectably religious of his day, whose words are all in favor of God, but whose life is opposed to him. We cannot escape the curious and disturbing fact that Jesus reserves his bitterest condemnation for people like ourselves: moral, righteous, religious men. This may well be the most important practical New Testament word on the meaning of sin. As if to make this denunciation unmistakably clear, Jesus declares that the tax collectors and the prostitutes

are closer to the Kingdom of God than the virtuous and
learned Pharisee! Is this because the tax collectors and prostitutes are secretly more virtuous? Not at all. Doubtless in terms
of what most of us would call virtue or morality the Pharisee
is far superior. He is a disciplined, spiritual man; honest, unsensual, moral. And yet this man is apparently excluded from
the Kingdom as he now stands, while the ceremonially un-
clean tax collector and the woman of the streets receive the
promise of the Kingdom as a present thing. Can we begin to
see the practical meaning of sin here? Can we understand just
what it is that Jesus is opposing?

" He also told this parable to some who trusted in themselves
that they were righteous and despised others: ' Two men went
up into the temple to pray, one a Pharisee and the other a
tax collector. The Pharisee stood and prayed thus with himself, " God, I thank thee that I am not like other men, extor-
tioners, unjust, adulterers, or even like this tax collector. I fast
twice a week, I give tithes of all that I get." But the tax collector, standing far off, would not even lift up his eyes to
heaven, but beat his breast, saying, " God, be merciful to me
a sinner! " I tell you, this man went down to his house justified rather than the other; for every one who exalts himself
will be humbled, but he who humbles himself will be exalted.' " (Luke 18:9–14.)

Here the distinction between Pharisee and tax collector becomes explicit and clear. The tax collector was concerned only
with his own sin; all that he brought to God was his own need,
his own recognition that he could not forgive himself. The
Pharisee was probably fully aware that he was in need of
God, but he was here guilty of that sin so tempting to the
religious mind: comparing his own relative lack of evil to the
relatively high degree of evil in others. Sin consists in precisely
this, Jesus is saying: our preoccupation with the evil of others;

the ease with which we notice the shortcomings of our neighbors or the failures of our friends; the very wide tolerance we
allow ourselves. It is almost true to say that the Christian is
interested *only* in the sin of his own heart, and claims no
special competence and no moral right to know how sinful is
the heart of either enemy or friend. All he knows is that sin
is whatever hinders God's access to him, and he finds that this
barrier usually takes the form — blatant or brilliantly subtle
— of self-centeredness.

The Christian is a sinner, a man who never fully escapes
from the tyranny that his self exercises over him. But he is, as
we have insisted, by God's grace a forgiven sinner. To give
full weight to both of these truths is the beginning of a true
Christian wisdom about man.

" It is a paradox that the highest and most spiritual view of
life which is available to man — and the one which carries
human beings to the most elevated and rarefied realms of experience — is one which starts with the assertion of universal
human sinfulness. . . . The finest examples of human saint-
hood and the finest blossomings of human personality seem to
emerge out of an abasement of the human being before this
very truth. They seem indeed to be inseparable from a con-
tinuous confession of sin, and the very power which works
with such efficacy in holy people is the knowledge of the forgiveness of sins. . . . Even if we pictured Christians as set
against the rest of the world, we should say that the Christians were the confessed sinners, not that they were the righteous arrayed against the wicked. . . . From the time of the
Gospels, indeed, it is precisely the self-righteous who are the
enemies of the spirit of Christ. And it is a pity that the modern
world has lost so much of the moral teaching which is to be
drawn from Christ's controversies with the Pharisees." (Herbert Butterfield, *Christianity, Diplomacy and War,* pp. 42, 43.)

Here is a final Biblical passage that may be useful in coming to a working definition of sin (Luke 7:36–39, 44–48).

"One of the Pharisees asked him to eat with him, and he went into the Pharisee's house, and sat at table. And behold, a woman of the city, who was a sinner, when she learned that he was sitting at table in the Pharisee's house, brought an alabaster flask of ointment, and standing behind him at his feet, weeping, she began to wet his feet with her tears, and wiped them with the hair of her head, and kissed his feet, and anointed them with the ointment. Now when the Pharisee who had invited him saw it, he said to himself, 'If this man were a prophet, he would have known who and what sort of woman this is who is touching him, for she is a sinner.'. . . Then turning toward the woman [Jesus] said to Simon, 'Do you see this woman? I entered your house, you gave me no water for my feet, but she has wet my feet with her tears and wiped them with her hair. You gave me no kiss, but from the time I came in she has not ceased to kiss my feet. You did not anoint my head with oil, but she has anointed my feet with ointment. Therefore I tell you, her sins, which are many, are forgiven, for she loved much; but he who is forgiven little, loves little.' And he said to her, 'Your sins are forgiven.'"

There are some difficult parts to this: some details of the hospitality of the day that need not concern us; some question about the relation between forgiveness and love. But the main point is surely clear. The true opposite of sin is not the rather formal correctness of Simon here, but the overflowing and almost extreme selflessness of the woman of the streets. She had behind her a life of sensuality, and she would always bear the marks of that life. But something had happened to her that prompted her to seek out Jesus, and something further happened when she found him. Her self-giving, her gratitude for one who accepted her as she was, this was her love, and seeing this, Jesus did that dangerous thing which caused so much consternation among the authorities: he proclaimed to her that her sins were forgiven.

In a deeply interesting and moving sermon on this incident, Prof. Paul Tillich has reminded us that we must not make the mistake of minimizing the woman's sin or minimizing Simon the Pharisee's righteousness. She was a prostitute; Simon was a righteous man, zealous for the law. The real thing we are asked to understand is that in this encounter Jesus stands with the prostitute and *against conventional righteousness*. The only righteousness that he recognizes as the genuine thing is one that springs from forgiveness. The woman of the streets had been forgiven; therefore she loved. Simon had not been forgiven; he didn't suppose that he needed to be. Therefore he did not love. This radical preference for Christian love above mere righteousness, this deep insight into the sinfulness of the world's good men — these are central in our Lord's understanding of the human heart. The only really good man is the forgiven man; the only real sin is the sin of thinking that you do not need forgiveness.

" Why do Christians turn away from their righteous pastors? Why do people turn away from righteous neighborhoods? Why do many turn away from righteous Christianity and from the Jesus it paints and the God it proclaims? Why do they turn to those who are not considered to be the righteous ones? Often, certainly, it is because they want to escape judgment. But more often it is because they seek a love which is rooted in forgiveness, and this the righteous ones cannot give. Many of those to whom they turn cannot give it either. Jesus gave it to the woman who was utterly unacceptable. The Church would be more the Church of Christ than it is now if it did the same, if it joined Jesus and not Simon in its encounter with those who are rightly judged unacceptable. Each of us who strives for righteousness would be more Christian if more were forgiven him, if he loved more and if he could better resist the temptation to present himself as acceptable to God by his own righteousness." (Paul Tillich, *The New Being,* pp. 13, 14.)

A regular study of such encounters as these, between our Lord and the ordinary men and women of his day, is one of the means by which we come to an understanding of our own selves, our sin and our possible dignity under God. When this rhythm of demand and gift, judgment and love, is really worked into the fabric of our religious lives, we find that it is no longer possible to worry about the other man's sin instead of our own. We begin to see that our consciences are never clear, and that the promise that they ever can be clear is a dangerous delusion. We begin to see that the one thing we can be absolutely sure of about ourselves is that we are sinners. And if we go on to say that "all men are sinners," we must be very careful not to make a practical exclusion of ourselves. We may say it of all men only when we first have been driven to confess it of ourselves.

But we do not say this kind of thing in order to show off our skill in confessing our sin. And when we call ourselves sinners we do not have any need to distort the occasional goodness that may be possible. To call ourselves sinners is not to say that we are not good; it is to say something far more serious. It is to say that we cannot save ourselves; we cannot make our lives whole by ourselves. Our own attempts to put ourselves in the center, we know, are abortive and certain to fail. We are sinners and we need to call upon God. To be a Christian is to come to need that call regularly and to come to expect that, if it is made humbly with a real and not a feigned contrite heart, God is ever ready to represent to us, again and again, his pardon and power in Jesus Christ.

SHIFTING THE ARGUMENT: MAN AND SEX

Is the picture sketched here of the Christian man as forgiven sinner a recognizable one? Do we see something of ourselves in it — something of what we don't want to see because it judges us, and something of what we want to see because it is desirable?

Is this picture true? And, even more important, is it relevant? Perhaps you are saying: " All right, this picture is probably true enough; it has enough of the conventional Biblical and religious words in it. But even if it is a more or less accurate picture of the Christian understanding of man, just how does this help me understand *myself?* "

Part II of this book will be an attempt to show that this Christian picture of man is deeply relevant to our needs. We shall turn our attention to the field of sex and, in our analysis of some of the problems involved, we shall try to show that many of the same basic insights into man's nature that we called Christian emerge out of a study of our sexual lives.

This is not a treatise on the problem of sex; it is an attempt to use the given facts of our sexual natures as a mirror in which we can see ourselves in a deeper Christian sense. It is an attempt to use something we all share, sexuality and its problems, as a guide to understanding the Christian view of man.

When we probe deeply enough into the problems of sex, we will find that we already accept as facts about ourselves much of what the Christian view of man claims as true.

It might seem ill advised to use our sexual experience as a means to understand the Christian view of man more clearly, especially since the Christian Church has not been particularly wise in its pronouncements and advice on this subject. Many assume that Christianity is not interested in the body, but only in the soul. Indeed, Professor Kinsey discovered that the stronger one's religious convictions, the less frequent was sexual practice, both inside and outside of marriage. Thus he was led to call Christianity a restrictive or repressive influence in sexual matters.

But it is possible to be too " spiritual " in religion. The Christian religion, at any rate, is something that ought to speak to the whole of life and to every part of man. Our study of the opposition of Jesus to the " spiritual " Pharisee and of his acceptance and openness toward the " physical " prostitute should have reminded us that the Bible does not simply identify the good with the spiritual, and the evil with the fleshly or material.

The dangers of too much " spirituality " in the name of religion can be illustrated by a passage from Alan Paton's novel, *Too Late the Phalarope*. Pieter, a young Afrikaaner, is speaking. His wife, like him a devout Protestant, is unable to love him in a complete physical way because of her inability fully to acknowledge that the body is good. This defect in her ultimately leads Pieter into a liaison with an African girl which becomes the center of the book's tragedy. Pieter speaks to his wife:

" It's all together, the body and mind and soul, between a man and a woman. When you love me as you've done, I'm comforted in them all. And when I love you as I've done, it's you I love, your body and mind and soul " (p. 87).

And later on Pieter continues, this time speaking to himself:

" And I wanted to cry out at her that I could not put the body apart from the soul, and that the comfort of her body was more than a thing of the flesh, but was also a comfort of the soul, and why it was, I could not say, and why it should be, I could not say, but there was in it nothing that was ugly or evil, but only good " (p. 88).

Perhaps our first step ought to be an attempt to correct the kind of falsely " spiritual " understanding of man that has been associated with the Christian view. Before we can use sexual experience as a pointer to deeper truths about the Christian view of man, we must ask this: What is the true Christian attitude to the body? Does the new self-understanding that faith brings include a distinctive way of understanding and affirming our physical life?

8

THE GOODNESS OF THE BODY

For the Christian faith, the body is a good thing. But just why is it that we find ourselves wanting to affirm this today? Is it because we want people to think that we Christians are all regular fellows like everybody else? Are we saying in effect, "Look, we can be just as frank, open, worldly, and sophisticated as you are?"

We must certainly watch our own motives here, as everywhere else. Our case stands or falls, not if it is gladly received or rejected, but only if it rightly renders the Biblical attitude to the physical side of man's nature. At the beginning of ch. 12 in his Epistle to the Romans, Paul writes: "I appeal to you therefore, brethren, by the mercies of God, to present your bodies as a living sacrifice, holy and acceptable to God, which is your spiritual worship."

Offering our bodies to God, he says, is part of our *spiritual* worship or service to Him. Why is this? The key here is in the little word "therefore." This verse stands at the beginning of the final section of the Epistle. I have already written to you, Paul is saying in effect, about the way God has acted in Christ to meet your sin and despair (Rom., chs. 1 to 8), and I have shown you how this activity of God works itself out in the whole drama of human history and destiny (chs. 9 to 11).

Therefore, what are you now going to do about this? You have a specific response to make, a particular service to render, a " spiritual " service, Paul calls it. One form of this response or service is to present God your bodies, the whole physical and material side of your life, that it may be used for him and not for yourselves.

But this goodness of the body is not simply true because Paul happened to suggest it at one point. Many other things he said we may find hard to accept. Must we accept him here? Let us look at two other approaches, which can help us confirm the goodness of the body in the Christian faith.

1. The first way might be called theological. Look at the whole story of the Christian faith, beginning in what we call heaven, moving down to earth, and passing up to heaven again. In this story, note the central role played by the body of man. In the accounts of the Creation of the world in Genesis, we find God looking at the different parts of the nonhuman world he has made and calling them " good." But when he looked upon the man and the woman he had made, he found them " *very* good." Christian thought has always been grateful for this primitive story, and has taken seriously its implication that because man is created by God, he is good. When, in the Genesis story, man " falls " into sin, it is not his body that is at fault, it is his will, his mind, his spirit — his desire to be like God. Sexual shame is not the source of man's sin in the story of the Fall; it is the result of a prior sin. In Genesis the body is made by God, and it is very good. T. S. Eliot has made the same point in " Choruses from ' The Rock,' " IX:

> " The Lord who created must wish us to create
>   And employ our creation again in His service
>   Which is already His service in creating.
>   For man is joined spirit and body,

And therefore must serve as spirit and body.
Visible and invisible, two worlds meet in Man:
Visible and invisible must meet in His temple;
You must not deny the body."

Further, the central Christian affirmation about Christ, the message of Christmas, is summed up in the statement that " the Word became flesh." Christians speak of God not merely influencing Jesus, not merely speaking to him in a vivid way, but of God becoming incarnate, making himself flesh, in the life of Jesus Christ. There are many other things that this doctrine of incarnation means. But it surely does mean at least that *the historical, limited, finite life of the body was deemed by God an appropriate place for his self-disclosure to man*. If the idea of God as Creator gives dignity to the body of man, the idea of God's incarnation in Christ further adds to that dignity. In the human life — body, soul, spirit, mind — of Jesus of Nazareth, God came into our midst.

We can discover in the sacraments of the Church further confirmation of the goodness of the material side of life. In our worship of God we are weak and fallible, needing reminders of a tangible kind. We cannot live simply by hearing religious words; we need to touch, to see, to feel. This is the kind of defense of the sacraments made by the Reformers, John Calvin in particular. In the Lord's Supper, for instance, we believe that in our eating of the bread and drinking of the wine, Jesus Christ is truly present to faith. There is here a rebuke of an excessively spiritual religion, another sharp reminder of the goodness of the material, physical side of life.

A final word on this theological approach to the goodness of the body. What about life after death? Will it be disembodied, spiritual, angel-like, or will it be a personal life in the body? Much of our talk in recent years about " immortality of the

soul " has implied that the body will be out of the pi<
life after death. Yet Paul and many of the Church's
talk about the resurrection of the body. Our grandparen
lieved that the very bodies that were laid in the grave would be
miraculously restored on the day of the Last Judgment. This
may be a crude position, and it is not accepted by many Protestants today. But it is nearer the truth than any view of life
after death that leaves the body out. We have very little evidence to rest our faith on here, but " resurrection of the body "
is a phrase that many people have been returning to and re-
interpreting today. By it they mean that in the world to come
our lives are not to be disembodied ones. We will not be
ghosts, but persons. All that we do through our bodies here we
will be able to do more completely " in that day " through the
new bodies given by God.

In the beginning, God looked at his creation and called it
good. At the end, God will give man a new body, fit for the
new life with Him. Much of our theological language in the
Christian tradition points to and suggests the goodness of
the body.

2. There is another way of making the same point about the
goodness of the body. Look at the picture of Jesus Christ in the
Gospels. Look at the accusation in Matt. 11:19 that he was a
glutton and a drunkard. Look at his concern for people's hunger, for their broken bodies as well as their distorted souls.
Look at his ministry, one not only of preaching but also of
healing. Look at the prayer that he offered to the disciples as
the pattern for all their praying: " Give us this day our daily
bread." Not, from some points of view, a very spiritual request
to make of God, but a deeply Christian one none the less, and
one confirming the many other ways in which Jesus displays
his concern for the bodies of men.

We have already mentioned the curious openness that Jesus

displayed to prostitutes and to all those whose life had been marred by what we call sins of the flesh. We noted his special tenderness toward this kind of person contrasting sharply with a certain harshness toward the perhaps unsensual but often self-righteous Pharisee. These facts will already have reminded us that the Biblical faith does not attach any special evil to the body. Man can sin with his body; he can turn this or any other part of him to selfish use. He can misuse any of the good gifts of God — his virtue, his mind, even his religion. But the body is a good thing; it is from God and belongs to him. Paul's exhortation confirms Jesus' actual attitude:

" The body is not meant for immorality, but for the Lord, and the Lord for the body. And God raised the Lord and will also raise us up by his power. Do you not know that your bodies are members of Christ? . . . Do you not know that your body is a temple of the Holy Spirit within you, which you have from God? You are not your own; you were bought with a price. So glorify God in your body." (I Cor. 6:13-15 19, 20.)

9

But Why Limit a Good Thing?

For the Christian man, then, the sexual dimension to life is good; no special evil can be attached to the body. Indeed, we have seen that in the New Testament the sins of the spirit are far more harshly judged than what we call sins of the flesh. The arresting statement by the fifteenth-century English churchman John Colet, "Pride is worse than a thousand concubines," is a faithful description of the Christian position.

But we must walk warily here. Even if there is no special sinful taint to body or sex, it is obviously true that man can sin through the use of his body. Body, sexuality, sex — these may not be the causes of sin; but the basic sin of self-love can certainly issue in sensual acts. We have only to recall the words of the Sermon on the Mount to bring this again to our minds: "You have heard that it was said, 'You shall not commit adultery.' But I say to you that every one who looks at a woman lustfully has already committed adultery with her in his heart." (Matt. 5:27, 28.) If we think carefully about sensuality, we will see that this sin of the flesh more often than not proceeds from the spirit or will. Beneath sensuality lies a more fundamental flaw.

We can see this by asking a question: What leads a man to sexual promiscuity? Not simply animal impulse, though he

sometimes defends the " inevitability " of his act by claiming
this to be the case. Often a person thwarted in the normal ex-
pression of his personality (one who does not find sufficient
chance to express his individuality in his job, in his family,
among his friends) will discover that a promiscuous sexual relationship can provide a sense of power and self-fulfillment
absent from the rest of his life. We can see at once that this
kind of promiscuity is not a physical problem at all; it is psychological or even spiritual, and the cure must be one that involves the whole man and not just his body. It is the whole
man, his " self " or his will, that is confused. In this way sensuality can be a way of affirming a self that is deprived of the
normal channels of self-affirmation.

It can also serve as a means of losing the self, of forgetting,
of withdrawal or retreat. Just as some who drink too much become noisy (ordinarily the ones who are quiet when sober)
and some become morose (often those who are quite jocular
and hearty when sober), so sexual excess can be both an attempt to affirm a frustrated self or an attempt to get away from
an overstimulated self. The man in a position of leadership,
called upon daily for decisions and action, looked up to,
drained of energy because of the pressing claims on his time,
his body, and his mind — such a man will sometimes seek by
means of sexual promiscuity to forget a self he does not like,
but which he is compelled by circumstances to adopt.

So there *is* a problem in the use of the body and sex. They
are good things, but they must be limited in their use. But the
question arises, Why limit the use of a good thing?

We have made it clear enough that we are asking the question of limitation because of the *goodness* of the body, not because of its evil. We are *not* saying that the body is an unfor-
tunate thing we carry about, that it ought to be treated as an
unpleasant necessity, that it has no Christian significance. On

the contrary, we are saying, because the body is good, because sex is a good thing, we want to see how this good thing can be used most creatively. We want to see, in religious terms, what it means to serve God with our bodies.

The whole argument up to this point can be summed up briefly. In Jesus Christ, God has done something for us that we could not do for ourselves. It doesn't matter whether you say that he has saved or redeemed or forgiven us, whether you say he has revealed himself or given us something of his grace and power. However you choose to describe what he has done, it is clear that this gift is something of overwhelming importance, if it is true. What are we to do about it? The answer is this: out of gratitude and obedience, we are to serve him in return. And part of us that must serve him is our bodies. To speak of limiting the use of the body, then, is both to deepen its significance as a good gift of God and to see it as a part of the Christian's religious life.

The "limit" that presents the greatest problem to modern society is the restriction of sexual intercourse to marriage. It is doubtful if premarital chastity, defined in this way, is specifically Christian in origin. But our problem is not to define its origin; it is to ask if it can be defended. And can it be defined and defended in a way that will illuminate the Christian view of man and his body?

It might almost seem as if it is too late to try. In many parts of our country today people experience only a slight moral shock when the bride of seven months delivers a "premature" child weighing ten pounds. This may be difficult for the child's grandparents for a while; but even they find other grandparents in the same situation, and it is soon forgotten. One suspects that we will soon be accepting as legitimate any child that is born in wedlock.

Professor Kinsey's figures confirm our feeling that we may

be looking for a defense of a lost cause. Among men 98 per cent of those who never went beyond grade school had some sexual experience before marriage; 84 per cent of those who never went beyond high school and 67 per cent of those with some college training had some form of premarital sexual experience. Among women the figures show an interesting variation: 30 per cent of those who never went beyond grade school had some premarital sexual experience; 47 per cent of those stopping at high school and 60 per cent of those with college training had some sexual experience. (These figures are carefully explained and analyzed in the reports by Prof. Kinsey and his staff. See *Sexual Behavior in the Human Male,* pp. 549–552, and *Sexual Behavior in the Human Female,* pp. 293–296. It might be added that Prof. Kinsey found that a fairly high proportion of the premarital sex relationships among women involved only relations with their fiancés before marriage.)

Christians and moralists, when they have spoken in defense of chastity, have generally relied on fear of conception and fear of disease as their major weapons. But this arsenal is running out, and these arguments are not very impressive today. Anyone really considering promiscuity seriously knows that with some care these fears can be almost completely eliminated. Parents presumably still urge chastity on their children as a form of obedience. But under the very real pressure of an actual situation, a parental maxim often will not hold up unless it has been thought through carefully and accepted afresh. A plausible defense of chastity is not necessarily going to arrest the sexual crisis of the Western world; but it is a pressing practical need. How shall we go about this defense? And, just as important for our purposes here, what can we learn from such a defense about the Christian faith and its understanding of human nature?

10

THE DEFENSE OF CHASTITY

Let us suggest three different approaches that might be used in a defense of chastity. To be useful for our purposes they must presuppose a realistic understanding of the nature of sex and be grounded in the Christian understanding of man.

1. *Sexual intercourse is an act of union in which each participant does something to the other.* This is what Paul meant when he declared that "he who joins himself to a prostitute becomes one body with her" (I Cor. 6:16). Dr. D. S. Bailey, in a very valuable book on this whole subject, spells out the meaning of this Pauline statement.

"Whenever a man and a woman enter freely into sexual relation, the principle holds good; their intercourse always makes them in some sense 'one flesh.' . . . Sexual intercourse is an act of the whole self which affects the whole self; it is a personal encounter between man and woman in which each does something to the other, for good or for ill, which can never be obliterated. This remains true even when they are ignorant of the radical character of their act." (*The Mystery of Love and Marriage,* p. 53.)

Our first line of argument, then, starts with Paul's realistic estimate of the effect of the sexual relationship on the participants. This is an act, a doing of something. It is not merely a case of the acting male and the passive female; both are actively involved. Further, it is not merely an abstract doing of something; it is a doing of something *to another person*. The result of this most personal of all possible relations, as Paul reminds us, is union: two become one — one body or one flesh. Every married couple knows something of this obliteration of the distinction between " you " and " me " in married love in general, and in sexual experience in particular.

Paul's further point here is that intercourse involves union even when the personal relationship between the participants is not taken seriously, even in casual and promiscuous sex. Union takes place quite apart from the personal attitudes of those involved. So, whether one likes it or wills it or not, sexual intercourse binds one to the other in an irrevocable way. The very act does an indelible thing; the future cannot blot it out.

Now what does all this enable us to say about premarital chastity? If sexual intercourse involves this union in one flesh, the act becomes dishonest if the union thus symbolized cannot be extended in all the areas of responsible life together. As Paul says, a man going to a prostitute becomes one flesh with her. But this is an egoistic, irresponsible, and incomplete kind of union. In it the man is actually saying that this union is not one that he is willing to carry through. He wants the pleasure without the consequences. So when the sexual act is entered into outside of marriage, it actually expresses more than either party feels. This is one of the sources of the guilt of the sexual libertine; the sexual act " acts out " real union, but the words and intentions of the persons involved deny it. And when gestures and acts begin to " say " more than inner intentions, and when this kind of self-deception continues for an extended period of time, something like disintegration of the personality can set in.

To sum up: sexual intercourse is an act of union in which

each person does something irrevocable and permanent to the other. Being an act of union, it can appropriately be engaged in only within marriage, where the actual structure and responsibilities of that union can be worked out and accepted. Only in marriage can this terrifying and demanding experience of union with another person be received and given without fear and guilt. To be the occasion for self-hatred, fear, and guilt in another is often the result of what at first sight seems only a physical act of promiscuity. Promiscuity is a profoundly spiritual act because in violating a person's dignity it can obscure the relation of that person to God. Sexual intercourse is a personal act that, often apart from our intentions, does something. It is strange, but in one set of circumstances — within marriage — it can affirm and enforce a deeply Christian attitude to human nature; in other circumstances the very same act can deeply violate that attitude.

2. *Sexual intercourse involves a kind of knowledge about ourselves and about the other person that can be communicated in no other way.*

This does not mean, of course, that some kind of objective information is communicated through sex. Perhaps a distinction between *scientific* and *personal* knowledge should be made. It is the latter kind we are concerned about here.

Let us imagine that a pretty girl moves into the neighborhood. She is in high school, and on either side of her live boys of the same age. How does each get to know her? One, let us say, begins to collect all the information about her that he can find: height, weight, former residence, and the like — all this without actually talking to her. It would be perfectly possible for him to collect quite a dossier of facts without speaking to the girl at all. And he would have, at the end of such a search, a kind of knowledge about her.

The other boy is not interested in this kind of knowledge

at all. He goes next door, rings the bell, introduces himself, and in five minutes of conversation he really " knows " the new girl better than his scholarly friend ever will. The first was dealing with scientific knowledge, the second with personal knowledge: not simply knowledge *about* a person, but knowledge *of* a person. It is with this second kind that we are here concerned. In what way, then, can sexual intercourse be said to involve an exchange of this kind of personal knowledge?

The simplest way of stating it is this: in the sexual act we come to know what it means to be a man (or a woman) and we also help the other discover what it means to be a woman (or a man). We discover, for the first time in a decisive way, the meaning of our sexuality. The uneasiness, suspicion, mystery, and sometimes fear, that attend much of the sexual side of adolescent and young adult life — this is banished by sexual intercourse. We know ourselves in a new way.

And, just as important, we know the other in a way we have never known another person before. Not new information; but insight into the deepest center of his or her life — what it really means to be a man or a woman. We know ourselves, here, when we learn to give ourselves; and we know the other when he or she gives himself or herself completely to us. Surely there is a kind of knowledge or insight here that is possible in no other way.

Now if it is true that sexual intercourse mediates a unique kind of personal knowledge, it is clear that a very special status must be given to the first experience of the sexual act. While, in a marriage, new things are always being learned about the other by a couple truly in love, it is also true that a decisive importance must be attached to the first time this mutual and intimate knowledge was ever shared. A man, for example, would seem to be bound in an irrevocable way — because of this interchange of knowledge — to the woman who first helped him understand himself as a man. Whether that woman was a prostitute years before his wedding, or his wife on their wedding night, the first encounter has a unique effect.

This seems to point to a strong argument for premarital chastity. The first sexual experience is so overwhelming and so different from any other experience that it is better reserved as a means of symbolizing and giving meaning to marriage. If man is bound in a permanent way to the first woman who shows him what it means to be a man, this is a strong reason for defining the sexual act as one that is possible, at its best, only within marriage.

3. *Sexual intercourse is a symbol of a relationship. Because of its nature, it can be an appropriate symbol only of a relationship within marriage.* That is the conclusion. Now let us see how it can be justified.

Sexual intercourse is not only a means of procreation, but also an act that can express or symbolize a particular sort of relationship between a man and a woman. We will need to clarify the phrase " appropriate symbol " first. If, having met you casually, I were later to meet you in Grand Central Station and throw my arms warmly around you, this embrace would rightly seem to you to be an inappropriate symbol of our relationship. Our actual relationship, being only a very casual sort of acquaintance, is not rightly depicted by my enthusiastic embrace. My gesture " says " more than our relationship warrants.

On the other hand, if I have been away from home for several weeks and on returning meet my wife at the front door with a cool how-do-you-do and a brisk handshake, that too is an inappropriate symbol of the relationship. In this case the gesture says far too *little*, expresses far less than the actual relationship itself means.

In other words, all of our physical acts and gestures carry a kind of built-in meaning, independent of the words we speak along with them. This is supremely true of sexual intercourse, which can express only a certain sort of relationship.

So we must look very carefully at the sexual act itself and ask of it, Precisely what does this gesture express, what does it symbolize? Doesn't it portray a most complete and radical kind of self-giving — complete commitment of one to the other, concern only for the other and not for the self? Humility, trust, selflessness — these are all surely implied in the act. Therefore, unless the act is entered into with the inner intent to show forth something of this humility, trust, and selflessness, it is inappropriately and dangerously used.

It can be claimed that marriage is the only social structure we know within which this symbolic act can be used. The act expresses too much mutuality, self-giving, interdependence to be appropriately used apart from marriage. Because it does symbolize or say all these things, when it is used apart from marriage, the participants know it is dishonestly used. The fear and guilt and shame that can spring from this kind of dishonesty can affect their personalities very profoundly indeed. Marriage is the only man-woman relationship that is able to contain the powerful meanings of the sexual act without injuring the characters of the participants. In marriage alone can we honestly verbalize all of the depth in the man-woman relationship that the sexual act symbolizes in gesture.

Thus, the symbolism of the sexual act requires the limitation of that act to marriage.

But what exactly does all this discussion of the body, sex, and chastity really tell us about man? How can it be said to illuminate the Christian understanding of man? Two general conclusions can be drawn immediately:

1. In the discussion of the goodness of the body, we have

noticed that the Bible refuses to make the body the chief instrument or source of human sin. We have spoken of the view that the body is something given by God, to be used for his service. Because through his body man is related to the whole of the natural world, the goodness of our own bodies can help us understand the very important Christian insight into the goodness of the whole Creation.

The world, historical life as such, is not evil; just as the body is not evil as such. The body as a good thing must be disciplined so that it can be most obediently offered to God. So the whole world of history and culture cannot be viewed by the Christian as something evil that we need to escape. It is something to be worked with, accepted, and when possible transformed so it can be a more effective place in which God's demands can be met and his purposes served. Our discussion of the goodness of the body, therefore, points to the true source for an idea of human dignity and to a true basis for a deep ethical concern for the world. Problems of hunger, housing, work, thus become problems of religious, and not merely political, concern. Anything that limits man's physical life unjustly, any social situation that denies his status and dignity under God, must be fought on religious grounds. If under God man's body and physical life are good, then no man and no institution that exploits other men or uses their bodies and lives in unjust ways can be tolerated.

2. Our discussion of chastity has reminded us of another part of the Christian truth about man. We are in fact tempted to use our bodies in irresponsible and self-centered ways. Our bodies are good, but they are also good things which we sometimes misuse. If the goodness of the body points to the goodness of God's Creation, our misuse of our bodies points to the equally fundamental idea of the " fallen " world in which we live.

We live in a fallen world, and we share as men and women

this fallen status. That is, we have been offered a high dignity by God and we have refused it. In short, we are sinners. If we were not, then an unselfish and disciplined use of our bodies would be the normal and natural thing, and none of us would be aware of any " problem " of sex. But sensuality is a brutal and commonplace fact in all our lives, even among those of us who claim to be respectable and to have avoided the more obvious forms of sensuality. Beneath the problem of sex, one part of which we touched upon in our discussion of chastity, lies a far deeper problem, the problem of sin. The body is not this problem, but it does show it up. The reality of sensuality (and the real difficulty we all have in convincing ourselves of the truth of self-discipline in sexual matters) points to that element in all of us which desires us to make our way through the world uncorrected and alone, with our eyes only on ourselves and our precious needs.

The goodness of the body points to and mirrors the goodness and dignity of all men made in the image of God. Any violation of that goodness or dignity, in personal or social life, is a violation of God himself and must be fought. The misuse of our bodies, furthermore, mirrors our sin and our self-centeredness. When sexual man describes his sensuality as something both infinitely attractive and repellent, the Christian feels the deep truth of this. For he knows that his faith can speak both of an exalted dignity and of a terrible depth in human nature. His own dignity and his own depth are clarified by his faith, and he is given a means by which he can recover the dignity and struggle against the radical wrongness.

In order to make as explicit as possible the fact that sex is not only a moral problem but a means of understanding the Christian view of man, let us turn in conclusion to three quite specific and central elements in the Christian's understanding of himself. In our final chapters let us look at (1) the problem of self-sufficiency, (2) the struggle between egoism and humility, and once again, (3) forgiveness. We have touched on all of these before. But our sexual lives remind us in a direct and poignant way that we cannot be self-sufficient; that we are indeed self-centered, but that we are fulfilled only by humility; and that forgiveness is a desperately necessary and freely offered divine invasion into the midst of our perplexity. Just how are these things true?

CHAPTER

11

We Are Not Self-sufficient

Perhaps the first thing that happens when we think carefully about the meaning of our sexuality is that we are reminded of our essential loneliness or incompleteness. The sexual drive is always a drive in the direction of another person. It can thus be viewed as a reminder of our lack of self-sufficiency, our need of another.

The greatest human need, we are told, is to be loved. If our parents have been successful, they will have loved us in such a way that we have become free. If we are successful as parents, it will be shown only if our love for our children has served to make them free of us. Failure comes when we have been wrongly loved, either by being deprived of it or by receiving a stultifying form. If we are not loved, we cannot love.

This fact that we cannot love unless we have been shown love is just another way of putting an essential fact about man: he is incomplete in himself. He feels alone, even in large groups. Being alone, he is tempted into all kinds of false escapes from his loneliness. Sometimes he flees to God in a neurotic way, using him to overcome his loneliness. Sometimes he flees to sex in a neurotic way; in this way sex can be a symbol of loneliness and it can also be a false way of overcoming and surmounting it.

Sex as a symbol of man's loneliness is implied by our earlier discussion of intercourse as a kind of union, in which two separate persons become one without destroying their own selfhood. Indeed, the union strengthens and deepens their selfhood. This incompleteness is externally symbolized by the mutual fitting together of the sexual organs; it is even more fully symbolized by the union of sperm and egg.

Sexually, then, man is alone, incomplete, unable to fulfill himself. But in the sexual life of marriage, such incompleteness and loneliness can begin to be dispelled. Here both the sexual act itself and the creation of a new life remind man that his loneliness can be healed only when an " other " enters the scene.

To be responsibly human, it seems, man stands in need of someone beyond himself. This is true of the sexual life, and it is also true of the moral and religious life. To show this, two points can be made.

The first is that *man is fully man only in relation to others.* Pure individualism is an impossible position. Secondly, the Christian would add to this " horizontal " point the " vertical " version of it: *man is fully man only in relation to God.* Let us look at these in turn.

The first point is perhaps the harder of the two to defend. What does it mean to say that I am truly man only when I fully come to accept my involvement with and dependence on other men?

I can have two quite different attitudes to the world that is " other " than me. I can think of it as somehow opposed, " out there," something which it is my task to overcome, control, and subdue to my purposes. This is partly a description of the scientific attitude toward the world, and it is an attitude that has produced many creative results. Or, on the other hand, I may think of the world as composed primarily of persons, like myself, to whom I must relate myself in a give-and-take way. My attitude in politics to nations or individuals opposed to me, my attitude to employer and employee, my attitude to my children — all these will be decisively affected by which of these two pictures of the world is dominant in my mind.

Both of these " worlds," the world to be controlled and the world to be lived with and accepted, are important, and we must all to some extent live in both. But is it not essential for the Christian faith to insist that the real world, the dominant picture, is that which puts personal relations at the center? This world is one I cannot control. I meet others and I cannot predict what they will do or say. When someone else contradicts, challenges, opposes, or limits me, I can either ignore, destroy, or come to terms with him. The real world in which politics, family life, Communism, neighbors, civil liberties, live is the world in which I am related to others as person to person. In this world I cannot deal with the other person as I choose. I must hear him, respond to him, meet his needs and adjust them to mine. Thus the real world is a world in which I am always contradicted, disagreed with, denied. Every other man is just as unique, just as free to take his own stand, just as much permitted to be eccentric and crotchety as am I.

Communism stands condemned partly because it cannot grant this; it cannot tolerate the existence of a world in which non-Communists are free to speak their minds and to act. To some extent both Roman Catholicism and Protestantism have forgotten this whenever they have tried to serve God by intimidating or legislating their opponents out of existence. American democracy is even now facing the problem of living together in the same world with those who radically deny its truth.

Many of us in our appointed work as scientists, workers,

housewives, spend a good deal of our time in the world of things that we can control. But all of us, whatever our profession, as men and women under God are thrust into the world of persons we cannot control. We must in this world reckon with " the other " in order to live.

That we are, in this sense, incomplete in ourselves is no unique Christian insight. Christians didn't invent the idea, and it is granted by many who are not Christian. But it is a fundamental part of the total Christian picture of man. Our sexual incompleteness can remind us of this truth, but it must be fully confirmed in the *whole* of our lives. We can be truly ourselves only as we accept as normal our encounters with others; with others who approve, accept, and encourage us, as well as with others who ignore, misunderstand, or oppose. " You shall love your neighbor as yourself " is the clearest possible statement of this fact.

Our sexual incompleteness can remind us of a second kind of incompleteness in man. Not only does life require other persons for its enrichment; Christians would add that man is incomplete without God. He is incomplete in that neither he nor any other person can be the center or source of the meaning of his life. He cannot " save " himself; he cannot, as we have already seen, effectively forgive himself. If a relationship to his neighbor is necessary for a full human nature, so is a relationship to God.

To be related to God, to love God, is more than a religious truism; Christians see it as absolutely necessary. One can almost say that man cannot be trusted to love his neighbor without loving God, for without God the neighbor becomes a means to man's ends, to be manipulated if he can be used, silenced if he is in the way. When man loves God, he comes to know what love means, and this leads him to see that his neighbor is, like himself, simply a man in need.

The sexual life thrusts man toward fulfillment in another; religiously this means that without God, who is other than man, he cannot be truly a person. *Man cannot be fully man without God.*

But there is a right and a wrong way of saying this. I may be tempted to make it mean that there can be no real moral goodness, no culture, no integrity, no honesty, no stability, apart from God as Christians conceive him. Thus all secular moral and cultural achievements are declared to be illusory and false. It is hard to see how this statement can be made without a very capricious distortion of the evidence. Even more to the point, it is hard to see how a Christian could make this statement without a terrible arrogance looming very close to the surface of his thinking.

And yet, *man cannot be fully man without God.* If there is any truth here, can it be stated without pride? Perhaps we do not know enough to say it about all men, but surely I can be permitted to say it of myself. I, at any rate, cannot be the man I should be apart from God. Not that under God I am the man I should be, but rather that without God I would be even worse. But even if we reduce the temptations to pride by making such a statement only about ourselves, we must still ask what it means to say even this.

It is often said that Christianity is a religion of salvation, and it is sometimes useful to point out that what it saves me from is myself. Without the God of Jesus Christ, I am left alone to struggle to be good. In this struggle, if I decide I am a success, I will become pleased with myself. If I decide that I am a failure, I will fall into despair and self-hatred. Neither in pride nor despair is there any hope; but, left alone, I have no alternative but to waver between the two. Without God I am just where Paul found himself, doing what I know I should not do, leaving undone what I know I should do.

Sometimes I become indifferent to this situation, sometimes I become guilty. But both guilt and proud indifference paralyze any real moral growth and make impossible any full manhood. Self-help books cannot help me get rid of myself. In the struggle against the tyranny of the self, do-it-yourself programs only make matters worse. I redouble my efforts to escape from myself either by going deeper into despair or by fleeing faster and faster into distracting amusements. But, at the end of my despair, as at the end of my distraction, the old self is still with me. I cannot escape it; I can do but one thing: I can give this self to God, admitting its frailty, admitting even its attempts to escape from him. What happens then is one of the strangest secrets of the Christian life: I become free. God can now make possible for me a new kind of self that I could not build alone. " Make me a captive, Lord," the hymn rightly says, " and then I shall be free."

This is what Christians mean when they say that they cannot know themselves, that they cannot discover their true selves, apart from God. Is this a way that Christians can say, " Man cannot be fully man apart from God," without claiming to be the sole custodians of all the wisdom of the ages? Christians have often been guilty of this kind of arrogance and, when they are, they deeply and rightly offend many who are wistfully wondering if Christianity has anything to offer. The Christian man does not claim to know very much. But he does know that without God he can neither understand nor deal with himself. He must learn to say this without arrogance, for an arrogant man speaking of God speaks of a God who is of interest to no one. Indeed, it is not truly God of whom he speaks.

Our sexual incompleteness, our need for an " other " in our sexual lives, has reminded us of two deeper and broader ways of saying the same thing about man. (1) We are truly persons only in encounter and meeting with other persons; the real world is a world of persons in which we are never allowed our own way. Part of a mature Christian response to the world is to accept this world of contradiction as one we can never escape. (2) We are truly persons only in encounter and meeting with God. He alone can save us from the despair that afflicts us when we look at our disobedience and folly. He alone can correct the self-importance and arrogance that always arises when we begin to notice too carefully our own unique wisdom, deep piety, and unselfish goodness.

Our sexuality reminds us of our incompleteness and loneliness. But neither sex nor any other human construction can be a true solution to that loneliness. To confess and offer it to God is the only way loneliness can be overcome and lived with.

12

OUR EGOISM AND HUMILITY

Sex illumines in a significant way the conflict between egoism and humility in the life of man. This is of course the key Christian conflict, and a Christian understanding of it is reinforced by our observations of the sexual life.

We have already seen how *egoism* of some kind is almost always the basis of promiscuous sexual activity. Man's self is at the center of this form of sensuality — either the affirmation of an insecure self or the attempt to lose and forget an overstimulated self.

Egoism is a temptation in the sexual life of marriage as well. One of the deepest meanings of the redefinition of adultery in the Sermon on the Mount is that it helps us understand that egoistic lust, akin to adulterous lust, may exist even between husband and wife. When one, ignoring the desires of the other, imposes or insists on the sexual act at a particular time, we can see that egoism is present even within the sexual life of marriage. Sex is one of the forms that egoism can use, in marriage or out, to elevate the self and lower or exploit another. The very thing we found to be at the center of the Christian understanding of sin — self-righteousness, pride, egoism — we can see destructively at work in our sexual lives. But if sex is a way that helps us diagnose and discern

74

our egoism, it is not a cure for it.

Strangely enough, our sexual experience also gives us an insight into the essential meaning and importance of *humility*. Even clearer than the way the sexual act reveals and embodies our pride, is the way it demands from us something like humility. It seems to be an obvious, almost physiological, fact that genuine fulfillment for both participants in the sexual act is possible only when each makes a special and careful effort to be concerned with the needs and demands of the other. When the man insists on his terms, his way, his timing, the act becomes quite incomplete for the woman, and vice versa. When such egoism is manifest, both the experience itself and the memory of it seem unsatisfactory. When egoism is overcome and a real concern of each for the other takes over, then and only then can there be a combination of physical and other-than-physical satisfaction. So one can almost say that we have built into our sexual structures this curious demand for humility. Unless the "other" is the important thing, neither will experience the greatest possible pleasure or fulfillment.

If humility has this curiously central place in the sexual life, we can look beyond this fact and make two important statements about Christian man in general. If humility is a condition of my sexual "knowledge" of another, (1) it is also a condition of *any* true knowledge of another person; (2) it is furthermore an essential condition of my knowledge of God.

These statements become less confusing if we remember that humility cannot be accurately defined as a simple willingness to serve others; pride and self-righteousness can serve others, and often do so. We have all been victims of the arrogant service of others doing something for themselves, thinking it is doing something for us. Humility is best defined as willingness to receive from others. This is where humility is required. For to receive anything from someone else — a gift, a service, a word of rebuke or affection — requires me to admit that I am not self-contained. It reminds me of what my egoism does not want to hear — that I am dependent on others.

Thus to know another person means that I must listen, receive, wait. Humility is a condition of my knowledge of others. I cannot learn about another person just by talking to him; I cannot truly know him by compiling facts about him. He must speak to me. He must " reveal " himself to me. But he will do this only if he feels that I am genuinely willing to listen and to receive. If he sees I am not willing, he will withhold himself. Some people listen to others only to wait for the end of a sentence to come so they can begin speaking again. This is not true listening; it is in fact merely another form of talking. Such self-centered listening will never truly know another person.

Humility is also a condition of our knowledge of God, perhaps the only condition. " The sacrifice acceptable to God is a broken spirit; a broken and a contrite heart, O God, thou wilt not despise " (Ps. 51:17). Biblical man understood this, and it has been seen throughout Christian history. When a friend wrote asking how he could come to know God, Augustine replied that there is but one way.

" In that way the first part is humility; the second, humility; the third, humility: and this I would continue to repeat as often as you might ask direction, not that there are no other instructions which may be given, but because, unless humility precede, accompany, and follow every good action which we perform, being at once the object which we keep before our eyes, the support to which we cling, and the monitor by which we are restrained, pride wrests wholly from our hand any good work on which we are congratulating ourselves. . . .

So if you were to ask me, however often you might repeat the question, what are the instructions of the Christian religion, I would be disposed to answer always and only, 'Humility,' although, perchance, necessity might constrain me to speak also of other things." (Letter 118.)

But what does it mean to say that humility is a condition of our knowledge of God? One thing it means is that knowledge of God, trust in God, or faith, can only come for us when we recognize what we can and cannot do in the search for God. Faith, and therefore knowledge of God, comes only when we stop storming the gates of heaven with our challenges to God to do something for us on *our* terms: defend Western civilization which is tottering; save us from the threat of Communism; give us peace of mind; make us good Americans. Now all of these goals are perfectly decent ones, but so long as we insist that we will receive God only when he satisfies us on these matters, we will never know him as he is.

For when God does come, it is to take over complete control of our lives. A man who only wants God to meet his own needs cannot allow this. There can be but one total allegiance for man; if it is not God, it will be some form of his own self-interest. Humility before God, then, is simply the dropping of any claims of the self, a willingness to fall into God's hands and to let him have his will.

We have seen the essential humility required in the sexual act, and we have been reminded by this of the twofold demand of humility that the Christian faith contains. We can know neither one another nor God without losing our pride and becoming humble.

There are two foundations beneath the demand for humility in the Christian life. One is the humility of Jesus Christ.

"As regards goodness, He was not conscious of possessing it himself independently, but looked away from himself to

God for it. When once a man addressed him as ' Good Master,' he replied: ' Why do you call me good? No one is good except God.' (Mark 10:17–18.) If we take the reply seriously, we shall surely find in it the supreme instance of that peculiar kind of humility which Christianity brought into the world. It was not self-depreciation: it was rather a complete absence of the kind of self-consciousness which makes a man think of his own degree of merit, and a dominating sense of dependence on God." (D. M. Baillie, *God Was in Christ,* pp. 125, 126.)

The other foundation for the humility of the Christian man might be called the humility of God himself. Was not God's coming in Christ the most radical kind of self-giving, or self-emptying as Paul called it? From the ignominy of the manger to the crown of thorns, we catch — through the humility of Christ — something of the character of God. We are called to humility as Christians simply because God has humbled himself for us.

13

FORGIVENESS AGAIN

We have already discussed the importance of forgiveness to a Christian understanding of man. Let us now see how our analysis of sexuality can further illuminate the meaning of God's gift of forgiveness to men.

Many Christian moralists approach sex with the single aim of urging some particular standard of sexual behavior on their hearers — marital fidelity or premarital chastity, perhaps. Now the case for fidelity and chastity must be made as carefully and persuasively as possible. But the Christian ought not to give the impression that he is interested in speaking only to the virtuous: to the chaste unmarried and to the faithful married. The Christian arguing for chastity and fidelity may perhaps be overheard by the unchaste and unfaithful. What then? A convincing defense of sexual discipline is likely to drive such people even deeper into the despair they may already know something about.

There is another Christian word to speak to the promiscuous that is more than a word defending chastity or fidelity. This is the word of forgiveness. Now this word, here as always, is a dangerous one. It seems on the face of it to undercut and make irrelevant the kind of defense of sexual discipline that we have been emphasizing. But there are none the less conditions under which it must be spoken.

To be sure, forgiveness cannot be received by one who does not admit his need. But if there is a person caught up in a sexual situation which both attracts and repels; if that person genuinely needs power to break through that situation and cannot find it; if there is a real desire for a fresh start and a desire to put the past behind — then the word of forgiveness can be received. It will not, when received, be mild or easy. Forgiveness is neither an easy thing for God to offer nor an easy thing for man to accept. The cross of Christ reminds us that forgiveness is not the same thing as the indulgent father's good-natured smile. To receive this word of forgiveness man does not have to become pure; he has only to admit his need. When he does admit this, God will enable him to hear the word of love and acceptance that always comes to the contrite heart.

But God will not let man stay as he is. He will begin to change man and make him over. This change is not a condition of forgiveness, but it is an inevitable result of forgiveness when it has truly been received. Notice how both loving acceptance and stern demand for change are present in the story of Jesus' meeting with the adulteress.

" The scribes and the Pharisees brought a woman who had been caught in adultery, and placing her in the midst they said to him, ' Teacher, this woman has been caught in the act of adultery. Now in the law Moses commanded us to stone such. What do you say about her? ' This they said to test him, that they might have some charge to bring against him. Jesus bent down and wrote with his finger on the ground. And as they continued to ask him, he stood up and said to them, ' Let him who is without sin among you be the first to throw a stone at her.' And once more he bent down and wrote with his finger on the ground. But when they heard it, they went away, one by one, beginning with the eldest, and Jesus was left alone with the woman standing before him. Jesus looked up and said to her, 'Woman, where are they? Has no one condemned you?' She said, 'No one, Lord.' And Jesus said, 'Neither do I condemn you; go, and do not sin again.'" (John 8:3–11.)

"Neither do I condemn you"—here is the meaning of the divine forgiveness. In the midst of our sin, God does not break off relationships with us; he stands alongside us in acceptance and love unconditionally given. But as soon as it is received, it makes a demand. It asks for obedience: "Go, and do not sin again."

There *is* a word of forgiveness for the sexually promiscuous, then. No version of the Christian faith can dare be too refined to forget this. But of course the pure need this word of forgiveness as well. There are forms of chastity that are merely technical and forms of marital fidelity that are fidelity only in the conventional sense. The sexually disciplined and pure, particularly such as may be self-conscious and proud of their virtue, will need to receive forgiveness for their pride. It may be harder for them to receive it, for it is harder for the pure to admit the need of God than it is for the prostitute filled with self-contempt. But the pure—even the loveless pure—can be forgiven.

A final reminder. To say that God's forgiveness comes to both the promiscuous and the loveless pure, means that there are none of us who do not desperately need it. The Christian understanding of forgiveness is not that it can be received only by prostitutes. It is that we are all as needy as was the woman Jesus forgave. And none of us needs forgiveness so much as the one who thinks he has no need of it. If any man can confront Jesus Christ and not be aware of his need, he has neither met the true Saviour nor looked honestly at his own heart.

When we begin to learn that we are in terrible need, God will come to us and begin to make us over into fitter instruments for his purposes.

When he comes, we will sometimes find ourselves saying, "It is a fearful thing to fall into the hands of the living God" (Heb. 10:31). But our final word will be the even deeper insight, strangely enough, of D. H. Lawrence:

"It is not easy to fall out of the hands of the living God for they are so large and they cradle so much of a man. It is a long time before a man can get himself away; even through the greatest blasphemies the hand of the living God still continues to cradle him." (Quoted by Samuel H. Miller, *The Life of the Church,* p. 82.)

This grace which includes both forgiveness and transformation is not only the Christian's hope, it is his faith. He has seen it happen in others and there is always the wonderful possibility that he will see it happen in himself and can give thanks to God.

In the revival of interest today in the Christian doctrine of man, the story of the "Fall" of man in Gen., ch. 3, has played a key role, influencing both the language and the ideas of much contemporary thought. It is important Biblical material on the subject of this book, and some readers may wish to look at it for themselves. But Gen., ch. 3, is not always immediately clear on first reading. The following notes and suggestions are offered as a guide to understanding and study.

Traditionally, the trickiest problem has been the issue between those who have interpreted Gen, ch. 3, as a true historical narrative about real people and those who have felt that the story is better described as a myth or legend or meaningful story. The fear of the first group is that you cannot call any part of the story true if it cannot be said to be historically reliable. The second group does not feel that it is necessary to believe that the author had in mind historical events and persons in order to maintain that there is a deep religious truth to the story.

Both of these positions are certainly responsible ones, though it will be clear that my approach here presupposes the second point of view. But, in any case, what the story actually means is more important than the issue of its historical or mythological character, and to that meaning itself we ought to turn.

BACKGROUND: GEN. 2:4–25

We should begin with a brief look at ch. 2, before we come to the story of man's sin itself.

God has formed man (in the Hebrew, *adham*) out of the earth or ground (Hebrew, *adhamah*) and has breathed into him the breath of life. Man is set in the garden to cultivate it, to work. But his labor is not the result of a curse, as it will be in the next chapter; here it is the thing for which he was made. He is permitted to use every fruit-bearing tree in the garden save the tree of the knowledge of good and evil. Should he eat of this, the Lord has said, man will " die."

But the Lord sees that man needs something more than a place to work (ch. 2:18). He is alone, and that is not a good thing. There should be someone with him to help him. So God creates all the forms of animal and bird life and offers them to man. And man gives names to the animals and birds. This is an important point, for to the Hebrew mind an object is not fully known until it has a name. Man seeks to understand the animals by naming them, we might say. But they do not serve him as adequate helpers; they do not overcome his loneliness. God sees this and gives man a true mate (ch. 2:21–23). The man names her, as he had named the animals before. Her name is Woman (Hebrew, *ishshah*) because she was taken out of Man (Hebrew, *ish*).

Notice that the names are still generalized, and do not yet seem to have the character of proper names. Notice also that in ch. 2:23 there is a second name for the man. First he was *Adham* or Adam — out of the earth. Now he is called *Ish*. Is the new name given because now that he is related to the woman he is really something quite unique and different?

In the final verse of the second chapter the author suggests that the man and woman have yet no sexual self-consciousness. They are naked and not ashamed. The stage is now set for the real drama to begin.

Ch. 3:1–7

" Now the serpent was more subtle than any other wild creature that the Lord God had made. He said to the woman, ' Did

God say, " You shall not eat of any tree of the garden "? ' And the woman said to the serpent, ' We may eat of the fruit of the trees of the garden; but God said, "You shall not eat of the fruit of the tree which is in the midst of the garden, neither shall you touch it, lest you die." ' But the serpent said to the woman, ' You will not die. For God knows that when you eat of it your eyes will be opened, and you will be like God, knowing good and evil.' So when the woman saw that the tree was good for food, and that it was a delight to the eyes, and that the tree was to be desired to make one wise, she took of its fruit and ate; and she also gave some to her husband, and he ate. Then the eyes of both were opened, and they knew that they were naked; and they sewed fig leaves together and made themselves aprons."

At the beginning, the man and the woman are innocent, but not completely. They must know what death is, or the threatened punishment would be meaningless; and they must also know the difference between obedience and disobedience. They have some sexual experience apparently, but they are not self-conscious about it and are not aware of its dangers.

The conversation between the snake and the woman is very interesting. The snake begins by trying to distort what God has said. Did God say, he asks, that you should eat from none of the trees? No, the woman replies, he did not say that. Only the one tree has been forbidden.

Next the snake tries to undermine the woman's confidence in the trustworthiness of God. He rejects at once the idea that she would die if she ate the forbidden fruit. Perhaps God made this prohibition out of jealousy, he suggests. So why should the command of a jealous God be kept? He is afraid that you will become like him, knowing good and evil. But isn't such knowledge a desirable thing?

The snake thus sets up a process of wonder and doubt in the mind of the woman. What she has simply accepted up to now she is made to question. Knowledge of good and evil? This would be a very desirable thing to have, she thinks. Besides, the fruit would be good for food and is very beautiful. So she takes the fruit and eats of it.

The key to the snake's strategy is his promise, " You will be like God." This is the temptation he offers. And this seems to be a real key to the writer's understanding of the nature of sin.

The woman, after careful consideration, eats the fruit. She gives some to her husband, and he eats it without so much as a question. It can be argued that the woman comes off better than the man here, although she is of course the first to eat the forbidden fruit. But we get the feeling that she has looked rather carefully into the whole picture. She has seen a number of reasons why the fruit should be eaten and she has weighed them all. The man has no such questions or hesitation. " Just like a man," someone has said of this; " all he does is eat." The early Fathers of the Church did not understand the admiration for the woman that lies behind this account, and through the centuries the story has ordinarily been interpreted in an antifeminist way.

The results of the eating are interesting. Perhaps they were expecting something terrible or wonderful. But what they do experience is merely unpleasant. They do not die at once; here the snake was partly right. Their eyes are opened; they learn how to distinguish good and evil, and — they discover their own nakedness. If death does not come from the eating, neither do they receive a Godlike omniscience.

A number of questions may be put to the story up to this point. What or who is the snake? Is there an answer here to the question, What is the cause of the first sin? If not, what questions does the story answer? What is the meaning of the tree?

Is there an answer to the problem of the origin of sin here? It seems to be difficult to find one. Why did the man eat the forbidden fruit? Because the woman gave it to him. Then why did she eat? The snake tempted her. But who or what is the snake? Are we to see the snake as the devil, the evil principle in the world? Then how did the snake become evil? Or again: Is evil a separate force apart from God that he cannot control, or does the snake as evil represent part of the woman's conscience as she wrestles with the meaning of God's prohibition? If the woman was innocent and pure and perfect, how did it come about that she could be tempted? Could she have been innocent if the snake was able to tempt her?

In his fascinating but difficult book *The Concept of Dread,* Sören Kierkegaard puts all these questions to the Genesis story. His answer is admittedly speculative, but it is very interesting. The woman was originally innocent, he said, but the effect of the divine prohibition, as she thought about it, made her anxious. She began to wonder if there were not a realm of experience, symbolized by the tree, that she was being denied. Her anxiety and innocence went along together until the tempter spoke, and it was because of this anxiety or dread that she submitted to the temptation to become like God. Reinhold Niebuhr, in *The Nature and Destiny of Man,* Vol. I, pp. 177–186, gives us a profound modern interpretation of anxiety as the occasion for sin that owes a great deal to Kierkegaard's position.

To attempt to find here a clue to the origin of sin is probably a fruitless one. It would seem that the story is really designed to answer the questions: What am I like? What is the meaning of my sin? Such questions as How did sin begin? or, Who sinned first? are really not answered.

As an answer to the question, Who am I? the story comes to life in a fascinating way. We can be intrigued by the details about snakes and women, but we mainly find that we read the story to understand ourselves. We too find that our greatest temptation is to forget our dependence on God, our obedience to him, our difference from him. We are the leading characters in the story.

This suggests an interpretation of the meaning of the tree in the center of the garden. Some have suggested that the eating of the fruit is a symbol of the discovery of sex. This seems plausible at first, for eating and nakedness are apparently closely related. But sin and sex are identified nowhere else in the Bible; God would hardly have told man to be fruitful and multiply in Gen. 1:28 if a direct connection between sin and sex were part of the Biblical teaching.

Perhaps there is a little more truth in those views which say that the eating of the fruit describes the awakening of reason in man or the birth of his conscience. In the garden before the snake arrives, this view holds, man is morally pure. He eats and loses his purity, but gains a conscience or a means of distinguishing between good and evil.

Perhaps this can speak most directly to us if we take the tree as simply the symbol of the difference between man and God. The tree symbolizes all possible knowledge. God is very generous to the man and the woman; he gives them a place to work, each other, and all they need to live on. But they want, for some reason, more than they need; they want to know what God knows. They want to be like him, to put questions to him, to call into question the basis of his authority. This desire is the chief sin of man. And as we have already seen, the rest of the Bible confirms this diagnosis.

Ch. 3:8–13

"And they heard the sound of the Lord God walking in the garden in the cool of the day, and the man and his wife hid themselves from the presence of the Lord God among the trees of the garden. But the Lord God called to the man, and said to him, 'Where are you?' And he said, 'I heard the sound of thee in the garden, and I was afraid, because I was naked; and I hid myself.' He said, 'Who told you that you were naked? Have you eaten of the tree of which I commanded you not to eat?' The man said, 'The woman whom thou gavest to be with me, she gave me fruit of the tree, and I ate.' Then the Lord God said to the woman, 'What is this that you have done?' The woman said, 'The serpent beguiled me, and I ate.'"

Now the Lord himself comes to the garden. He is walking in the cool of the day and calls to the man. The shame of the man and the woman increases when the Lord appears; they run into hiding, afraid because of their nakedness. The Lord hears the man confess his nakedness and knows at once that they have disobeyed his commandment. The Lord questions the man, who blames his wife. He even partly blames God: the woman, he says, whom you, God, gave me — it is she who gave me the fruit to eat. The woman blames the snake, and the destruction of innocence is complete. Instead of union and harmony between the two there is now guilt and accusation.

The time of peace and obedience and creative work is at an end. The Lord's response to this situation quickly follows. It is his curse.

CH. 3:14-19

" The Lord God said to the serpent,
   ' Because you have done this,
      cursed are you above all cattle,
      and above all wild animals;
   upon your belly you shall go,
      and dust you shall eat
      all the days of your life.
   I will put enmity between you and the woman,
      and between your seed and her seed;
   he shall bruise your head,
      and you shall bruise his heel.'
   To the woman he said,
' I will greatly multiply your pain in childbearing;
   in pain you shall bring forth children,
   yet your desire shall be for your husband,
      and he shall rule over you.'
   And to Adam he said,
' Because you have listened to the voice of your wife,
      and have eaten of the tree
   of which I commanded you,
    " You shall not eat of it,"
   cursed is the ground because of you;
      in toil you shall eat of it all the days of your life;
   thorns and thistles it shall bring forth to you;
      and you shall eat the plants of the field.
   In the sweat of your face
      you shall eat bread
   till you return to the ground,
      for out of it you were taken;
   you are dust,
      and to dust, you shall return.' "

Here the author describes the human condition of his contemporaries, and our own condition.

In the curse to the snake, there is the suggestion that up to this time it had either been upright on two legs or fully equipped with four legs. Now it is to crawl on its belly, to eat dirt, as it was then supposed that snakes did. Thus the author offers his interpretations of these facts or superstitions. He has also observed that women are afraid of snakes, and he adds that this fear is a result of sin. The early harmony between men and animals (the man had affectionately given the animals their names in ch. 2) is now broken because of man's disobedience.

If we can free ourselves from a too literal approach to this chapter, the problem of God's word to the woman becomes more manageable for us. To read this literally might suggest that the pain of childbirth today is caused by a woman's sin which she has inherited from the first woman. But a deeper truth is really involved here. Pain and suffering, the author is saying, do come from God, and they are often due to the sin of the world. We might want to add to this statement the conviction that this does not mean that suffering is good; it is still evil and must be fought against whenever possible. But here the author is touching on the deep truth of the relation of sin to pain in the life of man. Our own self-knowledge reminds us that our own pain and the pain of others is often caused by our thoughtless disobedience to God.

The second part of this passage involves the woman's subordination to the man. Now if we use this word to give a divine or Biblical sanction to a male-dominated family structure, we will be using it wrongly. Some have interpreted the passage in such a way, saying that it is God's will that the man dominate the woman, and that any struggle for some measure of equal justice for women is blasphemous. But it

does not appear that the author intends us to derive this from
his words. What the passage may mean for us is that man-
woman relations ought to be mutual and harmonious, as they
were in the innocence of the garden. But because of the sin
of the man and the woman, God proposes male domination as
a punishment. Such a plan is not God's perfect will; it is
God taking account of sin and disobedience and offering a
structure to keep it within limits. Because of his sin, man
tends to dominate the woman. This ought not to be, just as
sin ought not to be.

Interpreting these curses is very difficult unless we remember that the author is describing the human situation as he
sees it, relating the complex facts of pain and selfishness to
man's sin. Perhaps we should not be too certain that we understand the whole meaning of this section, and we certainly
ought to be especially careful that we do not claim that
Genesis gives us a full Christian understanding of man.

Finally, God condemns the man to work the soil for his
living. Before, the trees of the garden easily supplied enough
food, without any exertion on his part. Now the soil will be
difficult to work and will have to be tended with great care. He
will have to plant and harvest his food himself.

In conclusion, God says that man will have to die. Does
this mean that man was originally intended to be immortal?
Here, finally, the assurance of the snake is proved false. Even
if the man and woman didn't die at once after eating the fruit,
their ultimate death is promised.

Ch. 3:20–24

" The man called his wife's name Eve, because she was the
mother of all living. And the Lord God made for Adam and
for his wife garments of skins, and clothed them.

" Then the Lord God said, ' Behold, the man has become

like one of us, knowing good and evil; and now, lest he put forth his hand and take also of the tree of life, and eat, and live forever ' — therefore the Lord God sent him forth from the garden of Eden, to till the ground from which he was taken. He drove out the man; and at the east of the garden of Eden he placed the cherubim, and a flaming sword which turned every way, to guard the way to the tree of life."

Man is naturally alienated from God, the author concludes. This is a central fact about life. There is no possible return to innocence, whether of the garden, the womb, or of childhood. There is only the struggle to serve God in the world as we know it, here and now. This is a world in which there is great suffering and evil, but it is also a world God has made and continues to love. Man, shut off from innocence, must accept the world as he finds it, with both the evil and the possibilities for good that it contains.

We are reminded at the end of the story that all is not hopeless. To be sure, the man and the woman are expelled from the garden, but not before God takes time to replace their prickly clothing of fig leaves with softer and more comfortable garments. The very One who convicts us of our disobedience also comes to us with affectionate and tender mercy.